Cambridge Elements

Elements in Beckett Studies
edited by
Dirk Van Hulle
University of Oxford
Mark Nixon
University of Reading

EXPERIMENTAL BECKETT

Contemporary Performance Practices

Nicholas E. Johnson
Trinity College Dublin

Jonathan Heron
University of Warwick

T0364236

CAMBRIDGE
UNIVERSITY PRESS

CAMBRIDGE
UNIVERSITY PRESS

University Printing House, Cambridge CB2 8BS, United Kingdom

One Liberty Plaza, 20th Floor, New York, NY 10006, USA

477 Williamstown Road, Port Melbourne, VIC 3207, Australia

314–321, 3rd Floor, Plot 3, Splendor Forum, Jasola District Centre,
New Delhi – 110025, India

79 Anson Road, #06–04/06, Singapore 079906

Cambridge University Press is part of the University of Cambridge.

It furthers the University's mission by disseminating knowledge in the pursuit of
education, learning, and research at the highest international levels of excellence.

www.cambridge.org
Information on this title: www.cambridge.org/9781108737791
DOI: 10.1017/9781108767750

© Nicholas E. Johnson and Jonathan Heron 2020

First published 2020

A catalogue record for this publication is available from the British Library.

ISBN 978-1-108-73779-1 Paperback
ISSN 2632-0746 (online)
ISSN 2632-0738 (print)

Experimental Beckett

Contemporary Performance Practices

Elements in Beckett Studies

DOI: 10.1017/9781108767750
First published online: March 2020

Nicholas E. Johnson
Trinity College Dublin

Jonathan Heron
University of Warwick

Author for correspondence: johnson@tcd.ie

Abstract: How do twenty-first-century theatre practitioners negotiate the dynamics of tradition and innovation across the works of Samuel Beckett? Beckett's own tendencies towards fluidity of genre, iteration/ repetition, and collaboration – modes that also define the 'experimental' – allow for greater openness than is often assumed. Reading recent performances for creative uses of embodiment, environment, and technology reveals the increasingly interdisciplinary, international, and intermedial character of contemporary Beckettian practice. The experimentation of current practitioners challenges a discourse based on historical controversies, exposing a still-expanding terrain for Beckett in performance.

Keywords: Samuel Beckett, experimental, performance, embodiment, intermediality

ISBNs: 9781108737791 (PB), 9781108767750 (OC)
ISSNs: 2632-0746 (online), 2632-0738 (print)

Contents

1 Positioning the 'Experimental' in Beckett

Introduction: A Living Legacy

The year 2019 marked the first thirty years of Samuel Beckett's posthumous legacy, and as the world's theatres, publishers, and universities regularly, variously, and vigorously display, his literature is not yet gathering dust. Beckett's writing continues to find new readers, reach new audiences, and cross into new media. The complexity of his archival, philosophical, intermedial, and theatrical legacy generates new scholarship at a rate that few authors can match. Yet a discomfort attends this enrolment of Beckett in the literary canon, one perhaps signalled in the title of James Knowlson's authorised biography, *Damned to Fame*: how can avant-garde artistic innovation be preserved, once it becomes universally recognised and widely available? When undeniably epochal artistic work has left its epoch of origin, does it still function as advertised, or must it adapt to new conditions? In the 2060s, will received interpretations from the 1960s continue to domesticate the radicality of Beckett's vision? 'Habit', as Vladimir warns, 'is a great deadener'. How, in the face of ubiquity, will Beckett's thought live?

The problem seems especially acute in the theatre, which trades in ephemeral events, as opposed to the novel, which historically has taken the form of an apparently more static object (though literary forms too are changing within digital culture, and stasis may have been an illusion all along). Any Beckett performance in the era of late capital entails a collision between elements of the culture industry sometimes working at cross-purposes. Four of these 'agents' in the world of the theatre can be ranked on a scale moving from greatest to least 'degrees of freedom':

> Artistic impulse (what artists, given varying experiences of Beckett, wish to do);
> Production exigency (what is feasible to achieve within time, space, and budget);
> Market forces (what programmers/reviewers assume audiences will want to see);
> Copyright (what the Estate and its representatives will willingly licence).

Especially given the hard power vested in the latter two, such a system seems destined to lead to repetition over variation, or tradition over innovation. This might seem to suggest that Beckett is insufficiently available to contemporary theatre artists, or at least that his work is no longer a space of performative experimentation (if it ever was).[1] Compounding this perception is the reputation that Beckett (during his life) and his Estate (after his death) developed for

---

[1] The tension between the avant-garde and the canonical Beckett was noted a decade ago, in the lead editorial of the special issue on Beckett in *Performance Research*: '[to] the considerable, obsessive machine of "Beckett Studies" Beckett seemed at one and the same time too difficult and

reacting to controversial productions with legal action. Indeed, the partial list that follows implies a history of significant conflict between artistic impulse and copyright, with the 'calling card' of the conflict also listed:

JoAnne Akalaitis, *Endgame*, 1984 (setting)
De Haarlemse Toneelschuur, *Waiting for Godot*, 1988 (female)
George Tabori, all productions, 1980s–1990s (circus)
Gildas Bourdet, *Fin de Partie*, 1988 (pink)
Susan Sontag, *Waiting for Godot*, 1993 (text/stage directions)
Deborah Warner, *Footfalls*, 1994 (stage directions)
Robert Bacci, *Waiting for Godot*, 2006 (female)

Belying the prominence of these controversies in media reporting and thus in the public imagination, a far longer list could be made of work that did not meet with such restrictions, but proceeded nonetheless, despite falling outside of the theoretical boundaries. There is almost no prohibition that Beckett made in one case that was not transgressed in another, either with his permission or without his prevention. Partly on these grounds, we challenge the discourse that Samuel Beckett's drama is not already a terrain for experimental practice. This view may have developed from the series of historical controversies relating to the plays in performance, leading to a perceived restriction in interpretation or to limited freedom to experiment with Beckett on stage, but it does not reflect the complex and protean nature of such restrictions.

This introduction seeks first, then, to reclaim the experimental tradition within Beckett's lifetime, recalling how he interacted with trends in performance in the second half of the twentieth century, as he drew on, revised, and contributed to strands of both aesthetic modernism and postmodern dramaturgy. Beckett's use of generic fluidity, technology, long-term development, iteration, and collaboration – modes that also define the 'experimental', a term we discuss in detail later in this section – shows greater openness than is often assumed. Since his death, the range of practices happening at high-interchange locations and 'nodes' of Beckettian practice both continue and extend such innovations. The work of artists like Natalie Abrahami, Peter Brook, Katie Mitchell, and Robert Wilson, or of companies like Company SJ, Gare St Lazare Ireland, Pan Pan, and Touretteshero – among many others working in installation, festival, or university contexts – all reveal the increasingly interdisciplinary, international, and intermedial character of contemporary Beckettian praxis. Such experiments

---

too experimental, still, for the mainstream, but somehow too passé for explicit consideration by those at the "cutting-edge" of contemporary practices' (Laws 2007, 1).

enable engagement beyond Beckett, within wider social challenges and trans-disciplinary research problems.

What is at stake in considering experimental Beckett is more than simply an analysis of aesthetic choices or matters of taste in the theatre. This research is intended to open pathways where performance can be considered to illuminate contemporary culture. The multidisciplinary artists discussed in subsequent sections as offering examples of 'contemporary performance practices' around Samuel Beckett, both through their statements or through their work itself, articulate alternative modes of engagement and emergent features of Beckett's *oeuvre* that reveal new affordances for experimental research, performance, and education via his texts. Though this introduction identifies some of the experimental heritage of Beckettian practice during his lifetime, our main examples are drawn from the work of practitioners over the past ten years (since 2009), with attention to Irish and UK work that has demonstrated international impact.

We have in mind two audiences for this research. First, it is for scholars of Beckett whose expertise may (or may not) lie in contemporary performance, but for whom interpretation of Beckett's works in performance remains an area of enquiry; second, it is for artists, students, or educators who are seeking to update past models of Beckett in performance with attention to contemporary praxis. This intervention is not about staging plays, but rather about how twenty-first-century practitioners operate and negotiate the dynamics of tradition and inno-vation across the works of Beckett, including many works not 'intended' for performance or works not performed 'as intended'. In seeking to take a long view of questions that pertain to the past ten years of Beckett in performance and consider how they are relevant to the next thirty years of Beckett's recep-tion, this work groups experimental practices into three categories: embodi-ment, space, and technology. Before offering detailed case studies, however, this introduction proposes a theoretical and historical framework for the 'experimental' in Beckett.

'Accursed progenitor': An Evolutionary Model

In describing the situation that pertains to Beckett in performance now, we have found it useful to consider Beckett's literature as a living thing to which he gave birth. The discourse of literature is increasingly laced with organic metaphors, and Beckett studies is no different; indeed, Beckett scholarship is one of the driving forces in the wider field of 'genetic' criticism. The term 'epigenesis', invoked by Dirk van Hulle and others to refer to the post-publication/post-presentation alterations that individual texts continue to undergo, is useful in capturing the dynamics of change at stake here.[2] Biology uses the term 'phylogenesis' to discuss the evolutionary development and diversification of a species or group of organisms, helping us to group Beckett's texts as a phylum within literature that is undergoing collective change. We argue that Beckett's work today is 'evolving' – that is, his texts form living systems inherently connected to their origins, but also adapting to new conditions in a framework of multiplicity, according to a logic of survival.

A paradox is also involved in thinking about Beckett giving birth to anything, given his narrators' intense anxieties around parturition, obsession with birth trauma, and broadly negative orientation towards children. A recurrent theme in *Endgame* is the denial of reproduction or regeneration of any kind, for any species, precisely to arrest the inevitable processes of evolution: 'But humanity might start from there all over again!', says Hamm of a flea (Beckett 2006, 108). Of his own parents, Nagg and Nell, Hamm has nothing but invective to offer: 'accursed progenitor!', he calls his father (96). This is a layered accusation with biblical echoes (see Genesis 9–10 in the King James Version), and because of the passively voiced 'accursed', the subject here is ambiguous: it could refer either to the speaker of the curse (Hamm) or to a higher power. What is clear is that in a Beckettian universe, a primal curse attaches to the act of giving birth; in relating Beckett's writing to this act, it would follow that Beckett's writing is similarly cursed. These burdens are as follows:

(1) 'Born astride a grave': All writing is doomed to end; writers fade, works are extinguished, and the last reader who knows or embodies Beckett's work will someday die.
(2) 'A difficult birth': Writing is generally painful and difficult to create, for Beckett especially so. Doing justice to his writing, either editorially for publication or directorially for the theatre, is a challenge.
(3) '*Optimum non nasci, aut cito mori*': To be born is to enter into suffering, because of the machinery of desire. Writing, if it is truly alive, is by its nature unruly, unwieldy, and difficult to control; writing that survives longer due to its own excellence is, at the same time, ever more open to abuse and compromise.

It may even be that Beckett's 'lineage' or 'family' of works is specifically cursed, condemned to more difficulty than usual, due to Beckett's unique combination of talents and interests. Beckett exhibited prolific creativity across multiple media, but he was saddled with an extreme care for detail, the stress of

---

[2] A detailed exploration of epigenetics begun in *Modernism/Modernity* (Van Hulle 2011) is developed further in section 4 of *Modern Manuscripts: The Extended Mind and Creative Undoing from Darwin to Beckett and Beyond* (Van Hulle 2013).

which is exacerbated the more prolific one is. His strategy of 'vaguening' and his judicious use of silence, even his recurrent unwillingness to comment on meaning, paradoxically lead to a profusion and proliferation of interpretations. Quoted endlessly about the need to keep genres distinct, Beckett collaborated repeatedly and fruitfully on intermedial translations of his work. Famously resistant to the trappings of fame, Beckett's insights have resonated to such an extent that he is viewed almost as a secular saint. The theoretically rigid rules around acceptable performance choices are unevenly enforced, with the result that festivals, programmers, and audiences can't seem to get their fill of remixing, restaging, and rethinking this work. In short, though prodigious effort was expended during and after Beckett's life to exert control over the work, containment of an *oeuvre* is always-already impossible. Writing has an agency all its own. It may stretch the metaphor to the breaking point, but perhaps Beckett was a bad parent: limited communication, uneven rule enforcement, and attempts at control, followed by sporadic flashes of intolerance of his writing's hard-won independence.

If the basic idea of an organic paradigm for Beckett's literature is accepted, then this carries both political and practical significance for those who work in the field, either as practitioners or as scholars. Namely, our role becomes the construction and maintenance of a healthy ecology in which the work can flourish, expand, and continue to self-actualise, pushing the animating impulse of Beckett's work forward across boundaries and into new terrains. This is one of the motivations for establishing networks, conferences, research centres, and in our own case, the Samuel Beckett Laboratory, where spaces are designated and communities of practice are built that seek to address some of the questions that live within the work (Heron and Johnson 2017; Heron and Johnson et al. 2014). Such practice is conducted not in a framework of commercial endeavour, with the pressures of the culture industry that this entails, but rather in terms of iterative, durational, and fundamental research and pedagogy.

Living Laboratories: An Experimental Model

In the first dossier of outcomes from the founding year of the Samuel Beckett Laboratory, we cited Philip Zarrilli (2002) in relation to the 'metaphysical studio' (Heron and Johnson et al. 2014, 73). In the present introduction, in which we apply the words 'experimental' and 'laboratory' in the context of public and professional performances of Beckett, we again find Zarrilli useful:

> We should always engage the open-ended dialogical question of how our knowledges 'about', 'for', and 'in' continuously inform each other, and are not simplistically dichotomized. Our problem is to keep this dynamic

dialectic constantly 'alive', to have artists and scholars of performance join those scientists who are rigorously exploring the 'biological and phenomenological' and thereby building bridges 'between mind in science and mind in experience [Varela 1991, xv].' (Zarrilli 2001, 44)

This helps to map a relatively porous borderland in which the practices on either side of the notional scholar/artist divide are intimately related, perhaps because they are subject to the same societal forces and epochal events transforming the culture industries and universities alike. The debates that have created binary divisions between arts/sciences faculties or qualitative/ quantitative methodologies are called into question by the increasing priority on interdisciplinary research, social challenges, or transdisciplinary problems in which all are forced to engage. In the sections that follow, we explore Beckettian embodiment as an 'experimental entanglement' (Fitzgerald and Callard 2015, 16–23), an interdisciplinary methodology that brings the humanities and social sciences together with neuroscientific research to 'explore how different ways of being *experimental* can open up new avenues through which to think and work collaboratively across distinct arenas of expertise' (9, emphasis added).

The term 'experimental' denotes that which is *experienced*, tested, or observed, especially within the scientific context, where it is usually applied. Within the arts, the connotations of the term suggest the provisional, untested, and emerging (especially in relation to the avant-garde; see Harding 2013). Indeed, there is an etymological slippage at the root of the word 'experiment'. From the mid-fourteenth century, there is the 'action of observing or testing' alongside the 'piece of evidence or empirical proof', giving us the association with rigour and fact. However, there is a parallel trajectory for the word, from the Old French *esperment* ('practical knowledge, cunning; enchantment, magic spell; trial, proof, example; lesson, sign, indication') and the Latin *experimentum* ('trial, test, proof, experiment').[3]

This tension between the *enchanted/experimental* and the *tested/experimental* offers us a methodological opportunity, and not only for works by Samuel Beckett. It is tempting to associate the former with the arts and the latter with the sciences, but we suggest that experimental processes are considerably more

---

[3] 'Experiment' is in use from the mid-fourteenth century, according to the *Oxford English Dictionary*. The compendium *Online Etymology Dictionary* traces the origin in detail: 'action of observing or testing; an observation, test, or trial'; also 'piece of evidence or empirical proof; feat of magic or sorcery', from Old French *esperment* 'practical knowledge, cunning; enchantment, magic spell; trial, proof, example; lesson, sign, indication', from Latin *experimentum* 'a trial, test, proof, experiment', noun of action from *experiri* 'to try, test', from *ex-* 'out of' + *peritus* 'experienced, tested', from Proto-Indo-European root *per-*, meaning 'to try, risk', an extended sense from root *per-* 'forward', via the notion of 'to lead across, press forward'.

nuanced and complex than a simple distinction between the affective arts and the objective sciences. In most scenarios, the burden of proof lies with the practitioner of the experiment, or with the practice that claims to be *experimental*, which will always-already be some form of trial (even when the artist puts their own practice on trial). The fact that some notorious Beckett productions have migrated from the playhouse to the courthouse is a further 'trial' resonance here that we seek to rebalance. As Anna McMullan has argued, Beckett put 'theatre on trial' (1993) in his own practice, and we show that his later collaborators continue to do so, in acts of *enchanting* that seek to *test* the value of the texts through performance. While these contemporary artists are engaged in acts of *testing* through experimental practice, their source material is the original 'tried-and-*tested*' dramatic literature where we first become *enchanted* with Beckett. With McMullan, we also place this work within an interdisciplinary and intercultural research field. She writes that Beckett's works in performance are 'laboratories for staging embodiment' (2010, 14) that produce knowledge *and/as* experience.

'Beckettian experiments' may enter the public sphere disguised simply as performances of his plays; often, however, they appear within a theatre laboratory constituted as such, or they may be participatory events that encourage an audience to put Beckett 'on trial' through performance. Either way, the source text is being extended into a practical encounter that will enchant, test, or prove an aesthetic hypothesis through an embodied, spatial, and temporary activity. In practice, this happens in numerous ways and within diverse environments: from studios in schools, colleges, and universities, through to art galleries and public spaces. Some of these contexts may be experimental in the avant-garde sense, without being experimental in the rigorous or scientific sense. However, as several scholars of scientific experimentation have shown (Latour and Woolgar 1979; Crease 1993; Knorr-Cetina 1999; Barad 2007), this objective rigour is equally susceptible to the practical or *enchanted* knowing as it is to proven or *tested* evidence.

Robert Crease demonstrates that experimentation functions as theatre in *The Play of Nature: Experimentation as Performance* (1993), where he considers the stagecraft of scientific experiments. The laboratory as 'theatron' literally performs 'something materially into being . . . the laboratory itself is a space of action' and 'experimenters are in the role of producer-directors' (106). This interest in materiality of experiments is especially helpful for our study of contemporary performance practice on Beckett:

> Like artists, experimenters are restricted by the limits of their equipment and materials, they push these limits and must wait and see what works. . . . An artistic performance begins with a performative play-space that is not

> infinite. . . . A performer allows such things to function as organic parts of the performance as event . . . apparently inessential details spelled the difference between success and failure. (110)

That laboratories are spaces of failure – given Beckett's interest in failure – is also a crucial concept here, and several interdisciplinary studies of failure start to emerge, from science (Firestein 2015) to the arts (Le Feuvre 2010). Experimental failure is therefore an important feature of the aesthetic risk and the ethical value of our case studies. This work frequently happens within an avant-garde 'legacy' of failure ranging from Antonin Artaud to Pina Bausch, from Joseph Chaikin to Ariane Mnouchkine. Here creative failure is productive, generative, and *necessary* within experimental processes. For Chaikin: 'All prepared systems fail. They fail when they are applied. . . . Process is dynamic: it's the evolution that takes place during work. Systems are recorded as ground plans, not to be followed any more than rules of courtship can be followed' (1972, 21).

Staying with the historical example of Chaikin as an experimental Beckettian helps us to explore the practice of those selected later in this work. His published writing documents experiments in the avant-garde sense, but his interest in failure within laboratory processes also starts to address the scientific problems with methodology and analysis. Recent performance-based studies (Ridout 2006; Bailes 2011; Halberstam 2011) have tended to foreground the hopeful or radical potential of failure, which adopts an experimental strategy of *unknowing* to explore new terrain (see Heron and Kershaw 2018). Some of this work underpinned the ecological thinking of Gregory Bateson, whose paradigm that 'an explorer can never know what [s]he is exploring until it has been explored' (2000, xxiv) may resonate with experimental artists like Chaikin. His own reflections on his work with the Living Theatre, with Judith Malina and Julian Beck, and with his own Open Theatre ensemble, frequently use this language of exploration:

> Julian Beck said that an actor has to be like Columbus: he has to go out and discover something, and come back and report on what he discovers. Voyages have to be taken, but there has to be a place to come back to, and this place has to be different from the established theater. It is not likely to be a business place. (1972, 54)

The terms engaged here are reminiscent of Zarrilli's when he calls his studio 'a place of hypothesis, and therefore a place of possibility' (2002, 160). The question of whether the 'experimental' is the province of closed or open spaces – rehearsal rooms with fellow ensemble members and invited guests, or theatres filled with public audiences – is one of the tensions inherent in this strand of twentieth-century practice. 'Failure' as a term, of course, has different valences depending on what is at stake in the artistic encounter, namely how public it is.

And yet something productive emerged in the twentieth-century avant-garde from the willingness to fail in front of others: as Chaikin notes, 'when the Open Theater started we were only a private laboratory. We did performances, occasionally, but basically we were a laboratory performing unfinished work' (1972, 104). He imagined in 1965 that 'one of the good things is that we're willing to *fail*; it helps us go beyond the safe limits and become adventurers' (56, emphasis added). This fundamental kind of failure is a special joy of laboratory experimentation in both the theatre and the sciences, recalling Crease's conclusion that 'the artistry of experimentation, like that of the theatre, is often accompanied by a feeling of joy and celebration' (1993, 120). If this outlines the affect associated with *enchanted* experiments rather than merely *tested* ones, what are the circumstances or contexts that might give rise to this enchantment?

We argue that the key step is the revaluation of failure, as this encourages and sustains our natural curiosity towards the unknown (or provisionally unknowable). Failures to achieve *expected* outcomes that nonetheless teach us something, a normative concept in the sciences, is obviously a part of 'closed' performance laboratory praxis as well. But due to the material burdens of being a working artist within late capital, it is more challenging for artists/ audiences to embrace failure in the 'open' public cultural sphere of art practice. This is also why the term 'experimental' is sometimes used as a pejorative in certain regional theatre cultures or subsets of the theatre audience. Yet a fundamental association of failure with curiosity and creativity seeks to reclaim the term. The performance laboratory is a place of iterative failure, where artistic research produces an *unknowing* or 'not-yet-knowing' (see Borgdorff 2012) and where the distinction between 'things we *want to know* (epistemic things) and . . . objects *through which we know* (technical objects)' (190) emerges as a hermeneutic tool for experimental Beckett, especially regarding the tension between the enchanted and the tested indicated earlier in this section. We understand this tension as methodologically valuable to the tradition of Beckettian performance, and as an essential precursor to the emerging cultures of sustained/sustainable experimentation.

Performance Cultures: An Emerging Model

As the expansion of theatre texts and practices across national and cultural boundaries flourished in the twentieth century, especially in the related flows of 'globalisation' and 'festivalisation' towards the end of Beckett's life, a rethinking of what is meant now by 'performance cultures' is warranted. Since the 1990s, influential discussions in theatre studies began to identify the city (rather than the nation) as a key unit for such cultures,[4] and indeed it is visible how certain cities – London, Dublin, and New York – remain highly important 'nodes of practice' for Beckettian experiments. The examples selected for this research are predominantly focused around these high-interchange locations which both represent Beckett locally and distribute Beckett internationally. It is also noticeable that in all three cities, experimental works tend to emerge within a wider ecology of interested scholars, artists, and scholar-artists (and depend on the presence of a willing audience).

Our case studies, divided into experiments with (1) text and embodiment, (2) space and environment, and (3) media and technology, each have antecedents in the performance cultures of these cities, as well as among notable twentieth-century Beckett practitioners. Chaikin's practice, for example, is a clear instance of experimentation with embodiment and text: in his *Texts*, a piece mainly based on *Texts for Nothing* but including the closing lines of *How It Is*, he performed (1981) and later directed Bill Irwin in the same adaptation (1992), drawing together the intensely physical work of clowning with textual material that does not easily yield drama.[5] From the same New York avant-garde ecosystem of the 1960s–1980s, another prose adaptation like David Warrilow's *The Lost Ones* (1975) is an example of how space, by revising audience proxemics within an alternative configuration, can be used experimentally to generate new experiences of Beckett. Indeed, the whole archive of Mabou Mines adaptations (1976–86) (including *Cascando*, *Mercier and Camier*, *Company*, and *Worstward Ho*) reveals a thriving experimental culture that precedes (and, we argue, also supersedes) the legal crisis around 1984's *Endgame* at the American Repertory Theatre (ART) involving JoAnne Akalaitis.[6] For the experimental approach to media and technology that fills out the final set of case studies, we need look no further than Beckett's own practice as a key precursor. Beckett repeatedly 'iterated' his work with/on/ through media, generating alternative variations and foregrounding the technologies of distribution as well as philosophies of representation: Marin Karmitz's authorised film version of *Comédie* (1966) and Beckett's television versions of *Not I* (1977) and *What Where* (1985) all show an artist willing to

---

[4] See Kennedy (1993) for an early application of this model to Shakespeare; Fischer-Lichte (2009) and Pavis (2010) for a new discourse (and debate) around 'interweaving cultures' replacing 'interculturalism'; Harvie (2009) for a survey of theatre and the city; and Knowles (2017) for a recent survey of the whole literature in this arena.

[5] Materials relating to Chaikin's 1981 performance and the Chaikin/Irwin 1992 production were consulted at the University of Reading, which holds extensive 'Stage Files' on prose adaptations.

[6] Even Akalaitis herself went on to direct *Beckett Shorts* in 2007, transgressing genre (*Eh Joe* on stage) and bending stage directions/contract restrictions (mainly by interpolating music) without incident. See Goodlander (2008) for a review of the production.

reconsider his own admonition (written in correspondence in 1957) to 'leave genres more or less distinct' (Beckett 2014, 63).

Buttressed by the work of theatre historians and the substantial archive of performance scholarship within Beckett studies, we argue that experimental Beckett is also an 'epistemic culture' (see Knorr-Cetina 1999), where knowledge is productively blurred in processes that refuse the binaries of theory/ practice, thinking/doing, or archive/embodiment. Recent projects such as *Staging Beckett* (UK Arts and Humanities Research Council, 2015) have repositioned Beckett's work within 'contemporary theatre and performance cultures' (McMullan and Saunders 2018). The case studies we have selected extend and develop this work by investigating how Beckett is being embodied by twenty-first-century practitioners within the present *performance culture*. Though our key examples reflect evidence from the past ten years, the vocabularies we depend on to identify 'experimental Beckett' as such have been developed over decades by scholars, practitioners, and many who are both.[7] As Lois Oppenheim argues, directors of Beckett must grapple with 'a schism between the experiential and the aesthetic', and yet theatre also entails 'the metamorphosis of one into the other' (1997, 1). Thus, she goes on, the 'rendering of these texts in the theatre ... allows for an apprehension of the problem' raised by the 'intersubjectivity' of author, director, actor, character, and spectator (1). Over the course of our argument, we address this tension head-on, by focusing our attention on contemporary practice that experiments *with/on/through* Beckett in performance. While we remain focused upon embodiment, space, and technology, the practice under investigation is international, interdisciplinary, and intermedial, enabling a perspective that opens the texts up to post-dramatic or even anti-theatrical approaches. One need only consider the influence of live art practice upon the conventional theatre forms to understand how this might be generative and essential:

> Thinking about Beckett in the context of Performance Art enables us to reconsider elements vital to his theatre: the experience of the body in space in terms of duration and endurance; the role of repetition, reiteration and rehearsal; and the visceral interplay between language and the body. (Tubridy 2014, 49–50)

Without rehearsing the drama/theatre/performance spectrum here (see Shepherd and Wallis 2004), the experimental culture from which Beckett emerged is crucial to our study and has a highly significant legacy within the

---

[7] Especially influential volumes have included Cohn (1980), Brater (1987), McMillan and Fehsenfeld (1988), Kalb (1989), and Worth (1999), in addition to those we mention in greater detail within the text.

field: 'this spirit of open experimentation through performance is not a new movement or a fad; it is profoundly indebted to the work of many Beckett scholar-practitioners' (Heron and Johnson 2014, 8). One such scholar-practitioner was Rosemary Pountney, who continued to experiment with Beckett from her 1970s doctoral research to her 2010s performances, including her revival of *Footfalls & Rockaby* (2012) in Bergen, and a digital-durational project entitled *End/Lessness* (2017) produced by Fail Better Productions, in memoriam, following her death in 2016.

Another such scholar-practitioner is S. E. Gontarski, who has noted that: 'working with Beckett forces one to rethink the whole nature of the genre. Where is the theatre work, anyway? Whose work is it? It is Beckett's text, but whose theatre work?' (in Knowlson and Knowlson 2006, 258). Gontarski's ongoing practice *with/on/through* Beckett has included several adaptations of the prose works as well as new intermedial projects. His general reflections upon these processes have a specific resonance here: 'when Beckett is done paring down his minimal texts, how much creative space remains for other artists: actors, designers, and director? Or is there only one single artist in Beckett's theatre?' (260). His interest in the paradoxes of authority in the work brings forth an experimental opportunity that he contrasts with theatrical naturalism. He writes that Beckett:

> creates an ideological and aesthetic vacuum, which many a director and actor are all too willing to fill. It is a vacuum, however, that Beckett expects no one to fill, that, in fact, defines Beckettian performance, separates it from that of others. If actor or director fills that space, Beckett becomes Ibsen. (261)

To stay with that notion of vacuum, especially as it relates to experimental performance, we show how Beckett's texts produce a performative void, which still encourages aesthetic opportunities for artists working in any medium. For Fiona Shaw, writing at the time of her *Happy Days* but reflecting upon her *Footfalls*, 'Beckett had died only five years previously and I think there was still a great deal of sensitivity to any interpretative change. I remember the French co-producer saying with some panache, "Sometimes a vacuum is more important than a presence" – a generous theory given that their investment of £25,000 had just been lost' (Shaw 2007a). Within performance cultures, a vacuum or void offers a distinctive opportunity for practitioners working in the intersections between the arts and sciences, between embodied and digital forms, between 'pure' and 'applied' practice.

The hypothesis of an experimental method is that a body of evidence (sometimes theoretical) can predict an outcome in practice. Within the space of the laboratory, the experiment is given an epistemic location for the observation of phenomena (for the 'construction of scientific fact', see Latour and Woolgar 1979). The arts laboratory is sometimes a physical space, such as a studio, but primarily it signifies a process or event (Zarrilli 2002; Riley and Hunter 2009). In the sections that follow, we make the case through evidence of both processes and events that the experimental impulse, already present in Beckett's own twentieth-century performance ecology, is alive and well – that is, mutating and failing and going on – in twenty-first-century performance cultures.

2 Text and Embodiment ('First the body')

Introduction: The Biomechanical Body

If Samuel Beckett's literature is still alive, then this is because it exists within perceiving, enacting, and remembering bodies. Without a corporeal presence to extract thought from language, text on the page is a dead letter; without an audience to receive the sounds and images produced by performers, theatre is only rehearsal. Beckett's work has endured partly because he offered corporeal experiences to readers, actors, and audiences that were new for their time. It follows that the embodied possibilities within Beckett will continue to mutate and expand, as the meaning of embodiment continues to migrate and transform in the current century. This section explores the terrain of recent experimental engagement with Beckettian embodiments, thinking through how the assumptions arising from the performance tradition are being renegotiated for different bodies, as well as for new relations between text and performer, actor and audience.

This first section considers occasions when the body in performance subverts textual restrictions, whether through directorial interventions, performer innovations, or the body's being-in-itself. After positioning Beckett in the context of evolving models of embodiment as such, we note how such experiments can lead to divergences from text, yet also produce a specific – and sometimes enhanced – Beckettian embodiment. The examples begin with recent Beckett work by two practitioners best known for their innovations in the previous century: Peter Brook's *Fragments* (2008) and Robert Wilson's *Krapp's Last Tape* (2009). Extending from the same tradition but augmenting it with a renewed consciousness of gender and embodiment, various productions of *Happy Days* directed by Deborah Warner (2006), Natalie Abrahami (2014), Katie Mitchell (2015), and Sarah Frankcom (2018) are compared. More radically questioning the text/director, text/performer, and text/audience relation is the work of Touretteshero with *Not I* (2017), which is discussed in detail. The final example, pointing towards the work in the next section on space and environment, is the realm of dance- and movement-based exploration of

Beckett's texts, especially in the work of The Arcane Collective (a collaboration between Morleigh Steinberg and Oguri), in which 'intersemiotic' translations of Beckett's prose texts become fragmented and reproduced through embodiment alone. By considering these twenty-first-century productions, we show that Beckett's texts enable an experimental process of actor embodiment that frequently challenges how the audience encounters the play. By conceptualising embodiment as an 'invisible network' (Williams and Marshall, 2000) or a 'matrix of embodiments' (McMullan 2010, 126), we imagine Beckett in performance as an ecology of practice that extends the work into new aesthetic and phenomenological categories.

If Beckett's 'mimes and ... dramatic fragments constituted laboratories in which [he] tried out the possibilities of staging the body or a series of bodies' (McMullan 2010, 57), then these productions extend the meaning of the plays through innovative embodiments and 'experimental entanglements' (Fitzgerald and Callard 2015, 16). These embodiments are entangled because they depend on a complex web of interrelations between bodies, spaces, and technologies. To begin with, we should remember that these texts are deeply embodied literature, not only in the sense that we receive them and carry them within us as bodies, but also in the sense that they frequently represent embodiment (in detail). As Ulrika Maude has argued:

> Samuel Beckett's writing can be characterized as a literature of the body. There is a striking emphasis on seeing, hearing, smelling, touching, falling, rolling, crawling, limping, ailing and ageing in Beckett's prose and drama. . . . In its remarkable emphasis on embodiment, Beckett's writing distinguishes itself from the Western literary tradition, which has tended to emphasis psychological rather than physiological eventfulness. (Maude 2015, 170)

Beckett's educational experiences that exposed him to classical and Enlightenment conceptions of embodiment were formative for him, though frequently he engaged with such models (such as the Cartesian) in a mode of parody. Beckett's work reflects a shifting milieu and mode of attention to the body that coincides, even if it does not explicitly intersect, with both evolutionary and revolutionary changes in conceptions of embodiment across the discourses of biology, philosophy, history, and medicine during the twentieth century. Where this has most prominently manifested is the vitality of phenomenology, especially the mid-century work of Maurice Merleau-Ponty, which not only is central to the writing of Maude and McMullan, but also is engaged by practice-based researchers using Beckett to study the body. The so-called 'theory turn' in Beckett scholarship, perhaps most dominant in the 1980s and early 1990s but by no means ended, has yielded ongoing echoes and vocabularies that offer to name or critique forms of embodiment through interrelated branches of French philosophy: Beckett and the biopolitical, especially the work of Michel Foucault and Giorgio Agamben; Beckett and the body-without-organs of Gilles Deleuze and Félix Guattari; Beckett and the truth-subject of Alain Badiou.[8] As Sarah Gendron writes:

> Barthes, Foucault, and Lyotard are three philosophers who describe his work as teetering on the edge of modernism and postmodernism. The reason for this indefinite designation is different for each of these scholars, but they all evoke the idea of Beckett's writing as the embodiment of the *as yet unknown*. (2008, xviii)

Crossing from literary studies into theatre and performance, Beckett also showed an early preference for embodiments that were more 'physiological' than 'psychological', as is notable in his predilection for Buster Keaton and Charlie Chaplin, not to mention the more abstract branch of theatre in Ireland available in his youth: W. B. Yeats's dance plays, for example, he recalled fondly (Worth 1999, 132). His later theatrical work, especially after his own experiences as a director from the 1960s onward, strongly implies a pivot away from the psychological approaches to acting as well. Beckett was uncommonly explicit in a letter to Keith Johnstone, the groundbreaking British director and innovator of the 'impro' system, on 7 March 1958: 'a theatre stage is an area of maximum verbal presence and maximum corporeal presence' (Robbins Dudeck 2013, 39). Nothing is said here about the emotions or psychology of the performer: what matters for Beckett at the time, in advising a fellow writer about the theatre, is visibility (of what is on stage) and bravery (in continuing to write). When Maude invokes the figure of Darwin, she also places him adjacent to a key acting term:

> Beckett's writing captures a paradigm shift in our understanding of subjectivity, for since the second half of the nineteenth century, Darwinian thought,

---

[8] Naturally, the application of philosophy to Beckett has not been a one-way street. Sarah Gendron notes (with footnotes provided for each name, omitted in what follows):

> The ubiquitous critical engagement of Beckett with aesthetic theory and philosophy, and specifically as they relate to the modern/postmodern dispute about this work, also stems from the fact that Beckett's name and oeuvre circulated in some of the major philosophical discourses of his time. Georg Lukacs, Julia Kristeva, Jean-François Lyotard, Philippe Soller, Michel Foucault, Roland Barthes, and Theodor Adorno have all written about his work. (2008, xvii–xviii)

See Connor (2006), Feldman (2010, 2015), Fifield (2015), or the essays by Uhlmann, Weller, and Rabaté in Gontarski (2010) for nuanced reflection on how these philosophical 'adoptions' of Beckett can be thought in terms of Beckett's own philosophical tendencies, as well as their implications for critical methodologies within Beckett studies.

neurology, behaviourism and even some aspects of psychoanalysis had pointed to a *biomechanical* rather than conceptual understanding of the self. (Maude 2015, 183, emphasis added)

Theories of acting have exploited Darwin in various ways (see Roach 1985, 177), in service both to 'internal' and 'external' approaches to the problem of performance. Konstantin Stanislavski (1863–1938), who conceived of a theatre appropriate to the scientific age in that it progressed through observation, is most strongly associated with 'naturalism' in the 1880s and 1890s, and his vocabulary (though not always accurately or holistically transmitted) remains dominant in Western training systems and the public imagination.[9] Deriving from his branch is the received understanding of the actor's work as relating to sense memory, given circumstances, and believable representation. Vsevolod Meyerhold (1874–1940), often held up as a contrasting model, is more associated with Symbolism and the training system known as 'biomechanics', which he describes in terms comparable to Beckett's admonition to Johnstone:

> The art of the actor consists in organising his material: that is, in his capacity to utilise correctly his body's means of expression. ... Since the art of the actor is the art of plastic forms in space, he must study the mechanics of his body. ... By correctly resolving the nature of his state physically, the actor reaches the point where he experiences the *excitation* that communicates itself to the spectator and induces him to share in the actor's performance: what we used to call 'gripping' the spectator. (Meyerhold quoted in Braun 1998, 173)

His emphasis is on embodied memory (achieved through athletic repetitions), imagined possibilities, and engaging presentation. We argue that the history of acting theory in terms of Beckett suggests that his theatre offers a 'third way' of thinking about the body in performance, or rather an integrated and porous exchange between schools that are not as separate as they first seem (Johnson 2018). At the heart of Beckett's experimental practices with bodies in space, voices in text, and the technologies of representation, we see an opportunity to advance the study of performance and performer training through Beckett.

The first avenue of experimental Beckett we explore, then, is firmly rooted in both the physical performance tradition as well as innovations in directing associated with twentieth-century avant-garde practices. Robert Wilson (b. 1941), who embraces the descriptor 'experimental' in his online biographies although he is now one of the most lauded and established directors in the world,

---

[9] Many reception issues arose with Stanislavski's early texts that still linger, especially in the United States, due to partial transmission and faulty translation of his works, especially his incorporation into the project of what became known as the 'Method'. See Benedetti (2008, xv–xvii).

articulates an approach to actor physicality that is linked both to biomechanics and to dance:

> The first time you ride a bicycle, you have to think about what you're doing, but after a while you don't have to think about it so much. You can just do it. A friend of mine is a ballet dancer. I asked her how many ballets she knows, and she said, eighty or ninety ballets. And I asked her about something she does in Balanchine's *Symphony in C*, and she said, oh, I have no idea what it is I do, but when I'm doing it I know. It's in the muscle somehow. When she's done it so many times, it's there, it's automatic in the muscle. (2014, 106)

In 2009, Wilson premiered *Krapp's Last Tape* as both performer and director, his first major Beckett production (in 2016 he went on to direct *Endgame*). On a subsequent tour, the piece was featured at the first Enniskillen Happy Days Beckett Festival in 2012, Wilson's first performance on the island of Ireland. The performance was controversial among Beckett scholars, mostly because Wilson's heavy clown/physical performance aesthetic felt to many like a layer placed on top of the text from Wilson's own universe of images, rather than something arising organically within it. The production opened with twenty minutes of rainstorm, thunder, and increasingly ear-splitting noise, preceding Krapp's first line. Such a moment can be at the same time a 'consuming corporeal experience that is at once deeply pleasing to those pursuing live theatre as a physical-philosophical experience' and 'profoundly daunting to those seeking to understand *Krapp's Last Tape* for the first time' (Johnson and O'Connell 2014). It is perhaps emblematic of a director whose vision was always idiosyncratic, and whose practice creatively undermined text as a producer of 'sense' while prioritising the sensory.

An intervention with similar features – a world-renowned *auteur* director and the inversion or subversion of stage directions that are normally included in the rights contracts for producing Beckett – occurred in the work of Peter Brook (b. 1925) with his 2007 *Fragments*, incorporating *Rockaby* and *neither* (both performed by Kathryn Hunter) alongside *Act Without Words II*, *Rough for Theatre I*, and *Come and Go* (first performed by Marcello Magni and Jos Houben, including Hunter in the latter). Certain flashpoints where Brook's experimental vision conflicted with Beckett's textual precision are obvious: Hunter's *Rockaby* dispensed with a rocking chair altogether, rocking instead with her own body, and in *Come and Go*, which usually features three older women, two men (known in the performance culture for their clown-style work with Complicité) performed. These moves had their detractors as well as their conceptual justifications: honouring Beckett's subtractive theatrical logic and austere minimalism, the reduction of *Rockaby* to pure gesture nodded to the mime work elsewhere in Brook's series. In the *Guardian*, Andrew Dickson credited the performer (rather than the playwright) with bringing an embodiment to the text: 'she lends the text a gut-wrenching humanity quite at odds with its disembodied form' (2008). Though altering the sex of a performer is one of the main historical restrictions and is theoretically enforceable, Brook's cross-casting of two performers within *Come and Go* read more as an inclusive staging with three genderqueer/androgynous characters, juxtaposed in an increasingly ludic atmosphere towards the end. It seemed to raise more fundamental (and contemporary) questions about how we define sex, gender, and identity, especially in the metaphysical universe of Beckett's 'theatre machines' (Brook 1996, 58).

Variations on *Happy Days*

This section compares four recent European productions where the actor's embodiment of Winnie in *Happy Days* (*HD*) develops an experimental territory of identity, co-presence, and the performance of gender. The comparison demonstrates that Fiona Shaw, Juliet Stevenson, Julia Wieninger, and Maxine Peake engage with an experimental process of embodiment that also sometimes challenges Beckett's published stage directions. The play, a two-act near-monologue in which the first act finds Winnie buried up to her waist, then in the second act up to her neck, poses numerous challenges for actors, directors, designers, and technicians. Brook, writing in *The Empty Space* about Beckett as an example of 'holy theatre,' captures the core drama of Winnie's optimism: '[it] is not a virtue, it is the element that blinds her to the truth of her situation. For a few rare flashes she glimpses her condition, but at once she blots them out with her good cheer' (1996, 58). Variations in how directors may perceive such a burial, and choices to be made in how actors may enact their own 'optimism', 'cheer', and 'blindness' in the face of this 'condition', 'situation', and 'truth', open the floodgates to a range of experimental embodiments.

The first actor to play Winnie, Brenda Bruce, who was a reluctant last-minute replacement for Joan Plowright at the Royal Court, said that 'acting Winnie was a terrifying experience ... if you drop a line with Sam's stuff, you are lost' (Knowlson and Knowlson 2006, 164). Fiona Shaw agreed: 'I found my lines hard to learn. Images did not build in the mind, they disintegrated instead – Beckett's writing is all interrupted thought' (Shaw 2007a). While the actors concur that learning the lines is one of the central technical challenges with Beckett in performance, something less obvious arises from a consideration of *HD* in performance:

When stage directions are as plentiful as Beckett's, there is an implication that they solve the play. They don't. There are 150 pauses in *Happy Days*, and each has no meaning unless it is filled with imagination, tension or thought. It's this that makes rehearsing hard. Being technically meticulous is only half the battle. (Shaw 2007a)

While there are some parallels here with the hardship often associated with the role of Mouth in *Not I*, something else comes into play with Winnie, as we can observe when we study one of the few actors to have undertaken both roles, namely Billie Whitelaw.[10] As Knowlson and Knowlson record, 'Beckett changed the text after Billie Whitelaw had already learned the role and this put great strain on their usually close relationship' (2006, 172). They quote Duncan Scott:

> I told Sam that she had confided in me that she would rather be doing *Not I* again – which I found difficult to believe, in view of the terror she felt during each performance – but Sam said he too thought *Happy Days* was the more difficult play. (172)

As we show later in relation to *Not I*, contemporary practitioners are now using several strategies to counterbalance this 'difficult' performance history with more inclusive and collaborative theatre methods. One example of this is Abrahami's Young Vic Theatre production with Juliet Stevenson as Winnie:

> We did a lot of background work: gradually stalking, approaching the play, hunting it down. And with *Happy Days* we explored claustrophobia and buried Juliet in Regent's Park in the leaf pit there. Partly I was just really worried that what Beckett asks you to do as a director is put yourself in the role of a torturer. . . . I really wanted the [rehearsal] room to be a *happy room*. (Abrahami 2015, 253)

While this focus upon having a 'happy room' to go to a difficult place is a common pedagogy of rehearsal practice, this process did not shy away from intensely physical encounters with the physicality of the role:

> The decision to go to the Regent's Park leaf pit was to explore the claustrophobia and have it as a sense memory and also to create a more extreme situation to deal with so that then performance reality feels more achievable. (254)

---

[10] In recent work that rethinks Whitelaw's legacy, Zarrilli is critical of this tradition:

> Both the assertion that actors performing Beckett necessarily experience pain and the discursive fascination/fixation/fetishization on (mainly female) 'suffering', 'pain', 'sensory deprivation', and/or 'trauma' are sociologically and historically intriguing in terms of commonplace assumptions about acting and gender. I would argue that these discourses are problematic in that they occlude any attempt to analyse the experience of acting as a phenomenon or as a process where actors/directors/designers professionally problem-solve how to materialize a play's dramaturgy on stage in a way that creates as positive an environment as possible for the actor to accomplish her work. (2018, 100)

The rehearsal strategy of leaving the theatre and going into nature to engage with alternative embodiments or to prepare for the 'extreme situation' required in a role has a long history, but the presence of nature resonates especially strongly with the post- (or proto-) apocalyptic atmosphere of *HD*. As the play moves into performance, the central question of the text for directors and designers becomes: how will the actor embody the experimental interrelationship between scenographic design and the stage directions in the published playtexts? It is worth noting here, to return to 'epigenesis' in a theatrical sense, that the stage directions of a given published text are never wholly definitive of directorial choices, since Beckett often revised through his own theatre practice as self-collaborator, as documented in his theatrical notebooks and in the oral histories of actors, directors, and designers. Abrahami describes the design in terms of imminent nuclear apocalypse (in the 1960s) and climate change (in the 2010s). 'We started from the idea of someone being buried, buried alive by a series of landslides and then gradually created the rock face that those landslides would have come through' (255). This element in performance appeared both interpretative and experimental:

> The experience we wanted to create for the audience was that when they were to arrive at the Young Vic it would feel like they had arrived at somewhere like the British Museum and that you were viewing an installation where the last living humans had been found and they had been carved out of the rock and brought them and their environment back to be examined. (255)

Moving in the same world with strikingly different results, Katie Mitchell's *HD* (2015) premiered at the Deutsches Schauspielhaus in Hamburg, featuring Julia Wieninger as Winnie.[11] Mitchell's scenography, a domestic kitchen flooded with water (first to the waist, then to the neck), substantively revises the 'scorched grass' of the original, but seeks a kind of performative similarity, in that this element represents the audience's greatest and most current fear. For 1960s audiences, this was notionally related to the possibility of surviving a nuclear exchange; in the 2010s in Germany with recent flooding across Europe, the reference seemed to be to anthropogenic climate change. Mitchell was less concerned with the heavy symbolism of the space, however, than with

---

[11] As with Peter Brook, Katie Mitchell is a UK theatre director who practises extensively in Continental Europe. She draws upon the European experimental theatre legacy, especially Pina Bausch, connecting her with the Franco-Germanic tradition of Beckett to a greater extent than the Anglophone. She has been referred to (perhaps hyperbolically) as 'British theatre's queen in exile' (Higgins 2016); her work and influences are traced in a recent volume of essays edited by Benjamin Fowler (2018).

the impact of 'the terror of the situation' appropriately manifesting 'the real terror in the writing' (Mitchell and McMullan 2018, 129). Mitchell laments the legacy of 'artificial and mannered' stagings, in which 'the actor isn't really buried in the earth, you can see there is a gap ... that wouldn't be there in real life,' stating that this is a betrayal of Beckett's modernism: 'Winnie's cheerful refusal to face the reality of her situation only functions emotionally if we can see the horror of that reality' (129). What is, on the surface, a large-scale intervention in the stage image is not an artificial layer externally imposed, but is rather integral to the embodiment of the performer and how this affectively impacts the bodies who make up the audience.

The biblical echoes of 'the flood' and the uncanny impact of a design with hints of the Anthropocene recall Deborah Warner's 2006 production with Fiona Shaw, where the theatre space was opened up to the performance art *installation* or curated event:

> *Happy Days* didn't seem like a play at all, more an installation that talked – sometimes from the subject's perspective, sometimes as the voice of the subconscious. I kept remembering those lines from TS Eliot's *The Waste Land*: 'These fragments I have shored against my ruins' (Shaw 2007a)

As was the case with Mitchell, whose 1997 series *Beckett's Shorts* at the Royal Shakespeare Company had prepared the way for her journey towards *HD*, both Warner and Shaw had experience of 'installing' literature into performance environments, namely with *The Waste Land* (1997 and later) and *Footfalls* (1994), the latter being somewhat controversial for the Beckett Estate. That said, Warner reasserted her directorial authority with this *HD*, one of the first non-classical plays performed at Epidaurus, which invoked a different set of concerned authorities: 'This has caused a scandal in the press, with conservative elements asking why a modern play, particularly a Beckett play, should be staged in this ancient monument. What can it have to do with the Greek tradition?' (Shaw 2007b) This incisive question invites a discussion of tragedy for which the present study has no room, but of course the mimetic encounter between actor and observer remains as central to Beckett as it was to Aeschylus, Sophocles, or Euripides. Shaw predicts: 'As I look out from the stage at an audience not smaller than the population of a small town, I will think of Winnie's "strange feeling as if someone is looking at me"' (2007b).

This same line drew an anxious laugh from the audience at Manchester's Royal Exchange in 2018, where Maxine Peake was buried in a mound in a constant revolve and in-the-round. This eerie effect placed the audience in a comparable position to the protagonist, with the blazing light occasionally blinding our eyes as well as hers. Sarah Frankcom's production made some unusual interpretations in relation to the stage directions to accommodate this staging, especially in having Willie enter from the auditorium in Act Two. However, the most experimental implication of the staging on embodiment was the introduction of a camera, directly focused upon Peake's face throughout the second act, where the actor's ease with the televisual lens completely changed the tone of the performance. This shift from declamatory acting, spinning in a theatrical void throughout Act One, to an intimate, even voyeuristic tone in Act Two, opened up an apparently conventional production of the play to something bold and challenging. The audience's embodiment was also implicated in this shift, as we moved from an immersive position as *audience* members (*auditors* of a kind) to *spectators*, watching Winnie in close-up on multiple screens hanging above the mound. Peake and Frankcom's *HD*s therefore adapt the stage directions for an alternative dramaturgical effect, shifting the anthropological framework towards something more cybernetic and biomechanical: body as node in a technological network of organisms and screens.

Interventions with *Not I*

Touretteshero was co-founded in 2010 by Jess Thom and Matthew Pountney, inspired by Thom's experience of living with Tourette's syndrome. In the foreword to Thom's autobiographical book *Welcome to Biscuitland*, actor and writer Stephen Fry observes that: 'Jess's merry cry of "Biscuit, biscuit, biscuit!" [her vocal tics] delighted, amused and touched all ... the sight of her pounding her own chest [her physical tics] as she spoke caused many of us to wince in sympathy too' (2012, 4). In the company's first Beckett play, their 2017 production of *Not I* in partnership with the Battersea Arts Centre (preceding an Edinburgh run that summer and a longer London run in 2018), Mouth and Auditor created both fulfilled and enhanced versions of their roles, extending their embodiments into an experimental future for the play. Not only did the performers embody Beckett's 'buzzing in the brain', but the audience's bodies were also implicated in the event in unusual ways. The process has been documented in the film *Me, My Mouth and I* (2018), which was broadcast on BBC2 and BBC iPlayer. Challenging audience expectations about the 'embodied mind', Beckettian bodies on stage, and the phenomenology of Beckettian theatrical events, the performers inaugurated a corporeal 'matrix' that highlighted new and experimental aspects of the source text.

The neurodiversity of Jess Thom highlights the lived experience of the actor playing Mouth, as well as finding resonances with the character's own descriptions of verbal outbursts. This is experimental within the context of staging the play, which has competing relations to autobiography: first, because the scenography calls for the reduction of the body to a single body part, which could seem to result in the apparent erasure, lessening, or 'ghosting' of the actor's biography to an unusual extent. Second, however, the autobiography of a central virtuosic female performer has been frequently invoked in performance histories of the play – strangely, to an even greater extent than is usual with the much more 'marathon' *Happy Days* – perhaps due to the centrality of Billie Whitelaw's account: 'how is it that everything he writes seems to be about my life?' (Ben-Zvi 1992, 3). Touretteshero accepts neither a world in which Thom is subsumed within a stage image, given over to the text, and wholly forgotten, nor one in which Thom is reducible to her own background, experience, or story. Instead, Thom occupies the more Beckettian state of 'autography' (Abbott 1996) – writing the self – in a gesture that simultaneously elevates and effaces self-identity. That the play is *Not I* is thus a resonant and layered statement, a nugget of contradiction that Thom addresses head-on when she invites the audience to shout the word 'I'.

Thom's physicality is made both specific and enhanced due to the participatory event that surrounds the play, where the audience meets the performer out-of-role, alongside Charmaine Wombwell, who uses British Sign Language to play Auditor. Her 'peripheral listening' (Channel 4 2017) is a highly visible and embodied experience, encouraging the audience to engage with the text in a different way from the traditional still or silent spectator sitting in the dark. In addition to these unusual conditions, the audience's bodies are implicated in the event, through inclusive and non-conventional seating, shared use of lighting, and a sound design that plays contemporary music before the event begins. This environment, discussed in greater detail in the next section, is thus converted to a listening chamber, a communal ear like Epidaurus, a safe space in which to listen well.[12] During a relaxed performance in keeping with the ethos of the company, the audience are directly addressed and asked to move freely, to make noise if that is what their body does, and to come and go as they please. *Our* embodiment is therefore implicated in performance as much as the two performers on stage; we are in a shared space with communal values that are clearly articulated.

Some theatre reviewers have understood this production as a risky, participatory experience that fundamentally changes how we think about the play in performance. Thom's tics extend our experience of Beckett's text, and this *affects* bodies

---

[12] The phrase 'ear made out of stone and flesh' appears in Dickie Beau's 'Olden Lobes' speech, a video work that resonates with the contemporary political concerns of 2017 and highlights the degree to which theatre can uplift voices not heard elsewhere, presenting the voice of theatre director Peter Sellars (from 2015): 'The Greek theatre was a listening device that enabled you to hear a set of voices that were otherwise not acknowledged, and otherwise had no power. And a space was shaped on the side of a mountain next to the sea with this vista of sky, placing that invisible human being in front of you, and saying please listen. Please listen to this invisible person.' See www.youtube.com/watch?v=bIM1CPQD_4g (accessed 3 March 2020).

in the room. In an interview, Thom articulates her experience as follows: 'as someone who lives with that lack of control of language and that fear of involuntary language ... I feel there is a real resonance with the text. ... Mouth feels like a neurodiverse voice' (Heron 2018, 288). The embodied entanglement between Auditor and Mouth is at its most pronounced during the pauses in the play, where the performers share a repeated tic during Beckett's silences to recall the sound of Thom's body at rest (when she involuntarily tics). These restless silences feature both the word 'biscuit' and the physical tic of bringing the arm to the chest, which is mirrored by the Auditor. These paused bodies are never completely silent, which openly acknowledges the impossibility of Beckett's stage directions.[13] A performance history of Thom's body at rest, always overheard – *listened to* – during curated silences, is especially important when we consider the embodiment of the Auditor in *Not I*. Wombwell completes the text by reasserting Mouth and Auditor as a Beckettian pseudocouple, reminding us of the embodied network that connects mouths with ears through the phenomenology of sound. This Auditor performs sound as no other before her, literally gesturing the words (and tics) as a spontaneous, live encounter.

Touretteshero's work with Beckett has emerged from a deep engagement with the performative potential of Thom's tics: 'from this point on Tourettes won't be my problem – it'll be my power. From now on, I'm going to be Touretteshero' (Thom 2012, 7). Thom experiences 'physical tics ... deep inside my body' (43) and 'intense explosions of themed tics' (48), which involuntarily 'perform' her body in public spaces. When interviewed, she frequently states that the only seat in the theatre that she is 'allowed' to occupy is on stage, as her tics have occasionally caused offense during public performances and events. Her lived experience of theatre is one of exclusion; therefore, the practice of Touretteshero is profoundly inclusive in terms of both method and environment. They offer relaxed performances in accessible venues, and this conditions how they are *listened to* as experimental artists. Thom herself is used to being heard and *audited* in ways that sometimes prejudge her potential contribution to the space.

The experience of artists with disabilities and neurodiverse people within the cultural industries has been extensively discussed (see Kuppers 2014; Hadley and McDonald 2018), and Beckettian theatre provides resonant examples. While this particular production celebrates the reclaiming of a role mostly associated with virtuosity in the theatre, the implications for the plays that 'stage' disability merit

---

[13] Just as John Cage found that in a completely anechoic space, the noises of the bloodstream and central nervous system prevent any human body from experiencing or performing silence (1973, 13), Jess Thom's performance calls attention to the asymptotic character of silence in the theatre. The fact that she tics, and that her tics are signed by the Auditor during pauses, punctuates the performance with an intimately embodied form of non-silence.

further investigation and experimentation (e.g. *Endgame, Krapp's Last Tape, Rough for Theatre I* etc.). As recent interdisciplinary research projects such as *Beckett and Brain Science* (2012) or *Modernism, Medicine and the Embodied Mind* (2015–16) have shown, there is a wider opportunity for experimental performance to engage with medical and social models of body, brain, and mind. In the specific example of Tourette's syndrome, the *Oxford Handbook of Clinical Medicine* entry is quoted by Thom in her book: 'There may be a witty, innovatory, phantasmagoric picture, with mimicry, antics, playfulness, extravagance, impudence, audacity, dramatisations, surreal associations, uninhibited effect [*sic*]' (2012, 14). This clinical description captures something of the diversity and difficulty of Beckettian embodiment on and off stage. Ultimately, this is an experimental Beckett that remains open to contemporary culture, asking the bodies in the room for a different form of listening than is conventional with this text. *Panda* (2015) by US rapper Desiigner underscores elements of *Not I* (the pre-show and film components), another reminder that this is a twenty-first-century embodiment of Beckett. This production reclaims the text not only for neurodiverse communities, but also for a new generation, who may only have ever accessed Beckett online, if at all, and rarely on the page.

Translations in *Return to Absence*

Jess Thom's embodiment of Mouth – existing both inside and outside the text of the play *Not I*, constructing a self within a network of textual and corporeal associations with that text, and innovating with space, sound, and video to open a space around the text – point towards a clear model for experimental embodiments of 'para-textual' Beckett. Because only a minority of the time in the 2017 production of *Not I* was spent experiencing the text of *Not I*, a halo effect of Beckett-associated images, voices, sounds, and embodiments came into being alongside the performance of the Mouth–Auditor relation. A long heritage is invoked here again, of 'Beckettian' bodies in performance that are not specific to one text or necessarily part of 'matrixed' characters within a play, but belong nonetheless to the universe of Beckett and have a concrete impact on his living legacy. Beyond literature and theatre, every art form seems to contain examples where an artist has internalised some Beckettian sensibility and then externalised it in their medium. In the visual arts, a small sample might include Bruce Nauman (*Slow Angle Walk [Beckett Walk]*, 1968, based on *Watt*), Jasper Johns (etchings for *Fizzles*, 1976), or the Irish artists Sean Scully and Brian O'Doherty, both of whom reference Beckett across multiple works.[14] In music, often inspired by

---

[14] This extremely abbreviated list necessarily fails to capture the scale of the impact of Beckett on the visual art world. For sustained discussions, see Tubridy (2014 and 2018) and Reginio, Houston Jones, and Weiss (2017).

Beckett's own collaborations with Morton Feldman, John Beckett, and Marcel Mihalovici, composers have continued to productively engage with his works as source material, for example Stefano Gervasoni (*Pas si*, 1998), Damien Harron (*what is the word*, 2011), and György Kurtág (*Pas à Pas – Nulle Part*, 1997 and *Fin de Partie*, 2018).[15] Popular culture and serial television even get in on the act, turning Beckett into an in-joke for cognoscenti: the writers of *Game of Thrones* could not resist writing a scene in clipped, *Godot*-style dialogue for the actor Barry McGovern.

These are not performances of Beckett's texts exactly, neither are they clearly 'adaptations' of the prose or plays; instead, we think of them as 'intersemiotic' translations, following the work of Roman Jakobson in translation studies (1987) and Burç İdem Dincel in Beckett studies (2013, 2019). Jakobson, writing in the tradition of Russian formalism, articulates three modes of translation from text: intra-lingual (within a language, in different words), interlingual (between languages), and intersemiotic (from one system of signs into another, i.e. from literature to painting, cinema, or dance) (see 1987, 428–35). This notion helpfully expands the narrow scope of what is often meant by 'adaptation', since nearly every experience of a work of art involves translation, even when the notional 'fidelity' is to an original text. When Samuel Beckett gave permission in 1981 for the young, virtually unknown choreographer Maguy Marin to create *May B*, it was not to dance a specific work, but rather to generate an homage to his entire *oeuvre*. Rather than the solo female performance that an ostensible *Footfalls* reference might imply, the piece is written for a mixed-sex ensemble of ten. Writing of the dance's revival at the Enniskillen Happy Days Festival in the *Guardian*, Judith Mackrell notes how 'they're like a distillation of all Beckett characters, a community of derelict souls' (2015). The only text spoken in the dance is the opening line of *Endgame*; the source material is, in fact, the Beckett corpus.[16]

Thus, our closing example, as we reflect on the ways in which Beckett can be translated inter-semiotically and carried into the future via embodiment, comes from the world of contemporary dance. A piece entitled *Return to Absence* by the co-operative ensemble Arcane Collective (choreographed by Morleigh Steinberg and Oguri) was programmed at the 2014 Dublin Dance Festival. The festival's programme note, placed next to an image of bodies standing outdoors in greatcoats with bowler hats, is explicit that the piece derives from

---

[15] For additional detail on Beckett and music, see the essays collected in Bryden (1998) and Bailes and Till (2014), as well as two works by Catherine Laws: 'Beckett in New Musical Composition' (2014) and 'Beckett and Kurtág' (2005).

[16] *May B* (1981) is available in full online: bilibili.com/video/av10959949 (accessed 3 March 2020).

Samuel Beckett's *Three Novels*, saying that it 'inhabits the rich and peculiar realm of Samuel Beckett's trilogy, [embodying] the resonant images, wrought emotions and bleak humour characteristic of Beckett's world'. The choreography seems to reference the Butoh tradition, drawing out gestures with great slowness and intensity, and placing bodies in spatial dialogue with slowly modifying scenography (a large piece of paper-thin metallic plastic uncrinkling, for example). Other than fragmentary moments recognisable as birth and death, dressing and undressing, breath and silence, only a close reader of the novels (or an observer steeped in the Beckett performance tradition) might sense the connection to the source. The company's self-description online shows an affinity to the experimental in its articulation of crossing boundaries: 'With mesmerizing concentration and an urgent kinetic dexterity, the work of Arcane Collective pushes the boundaries of conventional contemporary dance with the uncanny ability to alter perceptions of the body, space, and time'. Such work advances the discourse, we argue, beyond the reductive terminology often applied to 'transgressing' genres as though the borders were real, and we ask again: 'can the culture arrive at a place where the Beckettian thought, regardless of origin or genre, is simply thinkable, or rather danceable, if that is the natural order?' (Johnson 2016). Responding to the spatial metaphor of 'bounded' works, the next section expands this question from the problems of embodiment and the performer to those of space, place, and environment.

3 Space and Environment ('First the place')

Introduction: Bodied Spaces

As Samuel Beckett's work moves through time and is embodied by new practitioners, the question of 'where now' (2010, 1) alters each fresh encounter, providing fruitful ground for new experiments with place, space, and environment. Both the bodies in question, and consequently the work itself, are marked by their relationship to location: the event of performance is changed at both the production and reception stages by local conditions, local politics, and local languages or accents. The heritage of Beckett in performance is rich in resonant contexts, arising at places and moments that seem to lend fresh weight to the work's content: San Quentin State Prison (dir. Herbert Blau, 1957 and after), Sarajevo under siege (dir. Susan Sontag, 1993), and New Orleans post-Hurricane Katrina (dir. Christopher McElroen-Pierce/Paul Chan, 2007) made three very different productions of *Waiting for Godot*. Even if the playtext were a constant variable – and archival, publication, and directorial histories suggest that texts are by no means constant over time or consistent across editions – then the people who are present at each given space and time, whether to make or to receive the play, are so marked by that context that place itself becomes an inescapable co-participant in the event. Just as bodies change texts by their own being-in-themselves, as shown in the previous section, place also alters the event, even when a source is 'faithfully' rendered. Referring to *Godot* in New Orleans, the *Guardian* review points out that

> So many lines reverberated with post-Katrina meaning – 'where are all these corpses from?'; 'there's no lack of void'; 'things have changed here since yesterday'; 'do you not recognise the place? Recognise? What is there to recognize!' – that the audience darkly chuckled throughout the entire show. (Brown 2007)

As a rule, then, it is possible to say that place matters and affects reception – a truism for all dramatic literature – but it is also reciprocally the case that performances *create* spaces at the moment they are defined as such: 'to say something is a performance amounts to an ontological affirmation, though a thoroughly localised one. What one society considers a performance might be a nonevent elsewhere' (Taylor 2003, 3). We argue that Beckett's relationship to space is qualitatively different and more open to experiment than other types of performance, due to his use of strategic voids. Beckett's 'vaguening' (Pountney 1988) and 'undoing' (Gontarski 1985) process – his elision of specific geographical place in some cases, or his contradictory onomastic references in others – create an ambiguity. When this ambiguity is placed within any non-ambiguous geographical location, it generates new responses and meanings in the text. If a writer's works occur in highly specific locations (as much of Shakespeare's work does, for example), contemporary theatre directors often 'strip down' or 'unbuild' these too-specific references as part of their dramaturgical work, in order to open up the fundamental and still-meaningful substrate of the playwright's thought to a living and present audience. In Beckett this work is often already done for us. However, this does not mean that the works are 'placeless' or indeed 'universal', since specific meanings are always generated in the moment of performance.[17]

---

[17] Though the full debate over universalism and Beckett is not engaged in the present study, it is worth considering again, given recent interest in the neurohumanities and the cognitive approach to acting, which sometimes suggest certain notions of a generalised model of *human* behaviour in the theatre, despite postmodern anxieties about an unthinking erasure of cultural differences. Zarrilli highlights the notion of 'constraints and affordances' at the heart of acting as a task, noting how it is imbricated with the issue of environment: 'the actor as a sentient being is focused on and immersed in the specific tasks/actions that constitute each moment of a performance score. In the performative moment, the actor is responding to the unique constraints and affordances offered by the text (if one exists), the performance score, the dramaturgy, *and the specific performance environment within which one performs* (2018, 102, emphasis added).

In comparing, for example, the specificities of performing Beckett in Dublin versus London or Belfast, the Staging Beckett project has noted the regional or local context of touring productions, leading to a focus on place as 'theatrical venue', which is always specific for the performance event. However, a further layer of ambiguity exists beyond the geographical: the theatre itself. Because the body in Beckett is contained by the scenography, the textual ambiguity of space also initiates a performance of place (Roach 1996; Taylor 2003). The examples in this section focus on the implications for the (actor/audience) body entering the performance from a geographical *location*, being *placed* into a scenography, and how that intersects with the construction of *space* by bodies in a performance venue. We therefore call that intersection *environment*, as we move through the different ways in which body and space interact.

While the examples that follow – drawn from the work of Pan Pan, Touretteshero, Gare St Lazare Ireland, and Company SJ – refer to their shaping of environments in a local context, it is notable that all four companies have extensive touring and festival experience. Since theatre cannot be as mass distributed as other media, many companies depend on mobility for survival, and much of this travel is towards festivals. A further experimental layer is involved in the collective spatialisation going on when Beckett is *placed* in either urban or 'destination' festival contexts. A festival, especially a single-author-focused 'Beckett festival', generalises the experience of Beckett across a great many bodies in contact with one another, creating a certain density of his ideas for that space and time (see McTighe and White 2018). The presence of a festival makes images, events, and experiences more nebulously 'Beckettian' throughout its duration: in Enniskillen during the Happy Days Festival, for example, a person walking through the town en route to a 'matrixed' Beckett performance might encounter any number of 'non-matrixed' incidents or possibilities of performance, and recognise (or produce) something Beckettian within these moments.[18] Wall graffiti appears that may or may not be a commissioned artwork quoting from *The Unnamable*; people in hats wait on a bench who may or may not be actors, and who may or may not be performing at the time; barbers and cafés along the high street adjust their menus ('Krapp

---

[18] Michael Kirby first theorised the distinction between 'matrixed' and 'non-matrixed' performance in the 1960s, to refer to the difference between consciously embodying fictional circumstances (i.e. acting a play in front of an audience) versus appearing in the same time frame/world as the spectator as a non-character-based performer. 'The context of place, for example, as determined by the physical setting and the information provided verbally and visually by the production, is frequently so strong that it makes an "actor" out of any person, such as an extra, who walks upon the stage' (Kirby 1965, 26). Though superseded in later performance studies by discussions of the 'postdramatic' (Lehmann 2005) and Richard Schechner's model of 'being' (existing), 'doing' (activity), 'showing doing' (performing), and 'explaining showing doing' (performance studies) (2013, 28), the distinction remains a resonant one.

Sandwich' being a particular favourite), starting conversations among locals with little previous awareness of the writer's legacy. By multiplying the spaces in which Beckett is produced, discussed, or explored over a short duration, festivals by their nature license experimentation in a way that the infrastructures of professional theatres perhaps do not always allow, in modes that no Estate could control. Brief common moments shared between theatregoing publics – the experience of waiting, for example – suddenly are transformed into tiny, high-frequency intersemiotic translations of Beckett. When considering research or community work that takes place within these environments, the density and dialogue between pieces is of use to us in thinking through the problem of *bodied places* in Beckettian performance.

Where the previous section noted the 'invisible network' emergent among performers and creative artists tasked with embodiment of Beckett, this section extends that network to encompass the senses of the audience, and to observe how in recent experimental performance practices, the audience's co-presence generates not only a 'node' of exchange with the artists, but also a set of non-matrixed performances for one another. In opening the frame to consideration of the audience, we are again drawing on the tradition of phenomenology, especially the aptly named *Bodied Spaces* by Stanton B. Garner. Garner states his aim:

> to redirect attention from the world as it is conceived by the abstracting, 'scientific' gaze (the objective world) to the world as it appears or discloses itself to the perceiving subject (the phenomenal world); to pursue the thing as it is given to consciousness in direct experience; to return perception to the fullness of its encounter with its environment. (1994, 2)

Garner returns us to the 'experiential duality' of the stage in terms of space: the objective realm of scenic space, objectified through semiotic analysis, versus environmental space, 'subjectified' and '*inter*subjectified' by the presence of the actors and audience (3). Joseph Roach, in his monumental study of 'circum-Atlantic performance', *Cities of the Dead*, extends the same metaphor beyond the theatre to rituals such as funerals, writing for example of the death of a king: 'there also exists an invisible network of allegiances, interests, and resistances that constitutes the imagined community' (1996, 39).

As different bodies slip in and out of texts, so texts and bodies slip in and out of places, and in these transactions, transformations are inevitable. As argued in the previous section, 'intersemiotic' forms of translation challenge any attempt to control Beckett's legacy as his texts/concepts spread through their re-embodiment in contemporary performance cultures. Similarly, experiments that involve 'non-matrixed performances' – watching a figure perform who is 'not acting' – and 'non-matrixed representations' – watching a non-acting figure who is consciously framed by certain representational elements – frequently subvert Beckett's precise control over space (see Kirby 1972). What interests us in this section are the new affordances, conceptual layers, and productive distortions arising from such experiments.

Bodies in Places: Moving the Audience

The disruption of traditional audience behaviours through environmental interventions has a long heritage. First, it is a strategy associated with some of the defined avant-garde movements of theatrical modernism, such as Futurism, Dada, and Surrealism, as well as linking to later twentieth-century practices of happenings and performance art. More recently, theories of 'immersive performance' in relation to theatre have developed to take account of the range of recent practices that involve active audience participation, as well as a variety of sensory (especially haptic) experiences in what has traditionally been a mainly visual medium (see White 2012; Machon 2013). This section looks at the impact of two companies, Pan Pan and Touretteshero, whose recent Beckett work touches on both tradition and innovation within the problem of how environmental and spatial interventions can combine to 'move' the audience (in all senses of the word).

A leading exponent of Ireland's theatrical avant-garde since the company's founding in 1991, Pan Pan Theatre has spent nearly thirty years seeking to live up to their name by maintaining a sense of liveness, tension, and exigency in both process and product.[19] Referring to this ethos in an interview with *Irish Theatre Magazine* in 2011, in which the company's new production of *All That Fall* was billed as something of a twentieth-anniversary celebration, director Gavin Quinn (who leads the company collaboratively with designer Aedín Cosgrove) said: 'It's always about ideas, and how we feel they will communicate to an audience at a particular time and place' (2011). This approach is explicitly contrasted with the more literary theatre that dominated Ireland at the time of the company's founding. Quinn discloses a broad spectrum of influences, ranging from the French art-theatre to the Polish avant-garde of the 1980s, saying that 'we started looking at all forms of theatre – theatre as an open form of expression in the usual way that an experimental artist would begin' (2011). The company explicitly drew on the relations between music,

---

[19] In radiotelephony, 'Pan Pan' refers to a signal of urgency (contrasted with 'Mayday' for emergency), suggesting that the station calling has 'a very urgent message to transmit concerning the safety of a station or a person, but does not require immediate assistance' (Government of Canada 2015).

visual art, and theatre to fashion its own performance vocabulary, moving gradually from the edges of the Irish theatre culture to its celebrated centre.

It is no accident that in the mix of peripheral, experimental, and difficult-to-classify artists central to Pan Pan's development, Cosgrove and Quinn found a strong link to Samuel Beckett, sufficient for Quinn to say that 'Beckett was always there' (2011). Both artists had worked on the first Gate Theatre festival of Beckett's plays in 1991, and both supported celebrated Beckettian practitioners in the early years, including Jean Martin and David Warrilow. However, from the perspective of post-2006 Ireland – after the year of Beckett's centenary and his attendant induction into the cultural pantheon of celebrated Irish writers – Pan Pan staging Beckett could seem at first like an inexplicable contradiction, or at least a mismatch. This was not, however, simply a sudden turn from the obscure Continental towards the canonical Irish; it was a far more complex negotiation of past and present, tradition and innovation. The terms of this negotiation echo, to some extent, Beckett's own paradox of place: How to be both Irish and European? How to explore the periphery while living at the centre?

Pan Pan's rereadings of older texts always highlighted the porous boundaries between visual art, sound art, theatre design, installation, live art, and performance. Their approach to Beckett was no different, and it did not emerge from a vacuum. After a visual citation of *Endgame* in their 2010 production of *Playing the Dane* (a remix of *Hamlet*), Pan Pan developed a Beckett series that has seen international and festival success since 2011, beginning with *All That Fall*, moving to *Embers* in 2013 and *Cascando* in 2016, as well as working with *Quad* in a lecture-demonstration that included a mathematics lecture and collaboration with ballet dancers. Their approach to the radio work (discussed in greater detail in the next section) has been largely to hide or disguise actors, but to place the audience in a specially developed 'listening chamber' or installation space in which their senses of sight, sound, and even smell are manipulated. *All That Fall* was fully recorded, but *Embers* broadcast live performers, semi-visible inside a giant sculpture of a skull, across a vast network of hanging speakers. The adaptation of *Cascando* built a giant maze through which the audience members, each wearing a djellaba and headphones, physically moved as a group. A revival of this production in Enniskillen in 2019 left the theatre behind altogether, letting its costumed audiences walk at sunset across fields near the Northern Irish border.

What becomes immediately clear when confronting these performances as a series is that the embodiment of the audience has been considered, and generally included, as an integral part of the event. 'Social sculpture', Quinn's term for the scenography of *All That Fall*, ideally captures the collapse of boundaries that Pan Pan's approach entails (2011). The body of the listener/viewer is no longer a passive recipient of art, but suddenly its active producer;

the bodies in the room perform for one another, non-matrixed representations (shaped and framed by the theatre-makers) within their environment. Sculpture becomes dissociated from its solitary and static tradition: the plastic work of art is suddenly networked, organic, dynamic.

In the case of Touretteshero, a different form of 'social sculpture' is at work. Long active in the relaxed performance movement in the United Kingdom, the company is strongly oriented towards making theatrical spaces accessible to any kind of body, and making this practice mainstream. In the social model of disability embraced by the company and theorised in theatre studies, it is inaccessible environments that are considered *disabling*, rather than the individual within them who is considered *disabled*.[20] So while the 'normative' audience–performer relationship is maintained in terms of space – that is, the audience for *Not I* is in one part of the room, their focus notionally on the 'stage' ahead of them – there is considerable freedom in relation to the attitude of the body ('standing, or sitting, or kneeling, or lying', as Mouth relates it) and to the actions that the body might undertake, whether voluntarily or involuntarily. Thus, there are participatory and inclusive dimensions to the staging of *Not I* as a relaxed performance that sharply contrast with the reverent atmosphere of silence and darkness in which the play is often insistently received: suffice to say that the Royal Court productions of *Not I* in 2013 did not include baby-friendly performances, as the Battersea Arts Centre programmed with Touretteshero in 2017. The Touretteshero work is therefore audience-responsive and inclusive, merely by shifting its centre of values – with maximal accessibility for all audiences uppermost – and engaging the environment to manifest that orientation. At the practical level, this means that instead of fixed seating, the room has movable dark foam and cushions. The performer is visible on stage from the beginning, directly addressing and welcoming the audience. Context and explanations that actively request, and then permit, whatever embodied responses may arise from the assembly frame the play's performance.

A participatory and immersive experience for Beckett audiences returns our focus to different questions, perhaps, but no less Beckettian ones: What kind of human bodies are empowered by certain spaces? Which environments will push our bodies and dislocate our senses? What impact do these containers and configurations have on our embodiments? These curated interventions come with their own duty of care, an obligation to prepare the audience for a challenge. Each company handles this differently, offering limited agencies to their audiences in different spheres, but the priority for both remains highly

---

[20] For additional context, see Kuppers (2013), Hadley (2014), and Hadley and McDonald (2018).

audience-aware and audience-responsive, at the same time as they develop and expand the scenographic and environmental legacies of Beckett's texts.

Places through Bodies: Site-Responsive Performance

When an audience network is carefully cultivated and then placed within a spatial matrix of immersion, site-responsiveness, or site-specificity, a further layer or experimentation with environment is activated.[21] The examples discussed in this section – pieces by Company SJ and Gare St Lazare Ireland – foreground site-responsiveness while retaining both the centrality of embodiment and the qualities of audience-responsiveness that mark contemporary performance aesthetics, especially in the recent Irish context. Such work responds to a substantial trend in twenty-first-century Irish theatre towards performances in alternative spaces, as part of a broad-based cultural reclamation of public environments and a reconsideration of the power relations that such architectures imply. The historical context for such work in the Republic of Ireland is dramatic: first, the 1990s, marked by the decline of the Catholic Church as a dominant social and state power; second, 1995–2008, the 'Celtic Tiger' era of unprecedented eco-nomic growth and wealth in the state; third, the 2010s, in the aftershock of the crash and subsequent recession, in which (among other social issues) state budgets supporting individual artists, theatre companies, and venues were slashed. Artists from all over the island – companies including Corcadorca, Performance Corporation, Siamsa Tíre, and WillFredd Theatre, as well as individual experimental directors like Marc Atkinson, Olwen Fouéré, Selina Cartmell, and Maeve Stone – built up individual credits (and sometimes company profiles) by intervening in public spaces, often with the contextualising support of the island's many festivals. The work of ANU Productions, especially the *Monto Cycle* (2010–14) that renegotiated both charged historical locations in the Dublin city centre (such as a former Magdalene laundry) and what Marc Augé calls 'non-places' in the urban landscape (departure lounges, roads, hotels, waiting rooms), is possibly the best-known example of this trend.[22]

---

[21] The precise taxonomies of site-specificity (see Kaye 2000; Wilkie 2002; Pearson 2010) and immersion (see White 2012; Machon 2013) in theatre are disputed; we have opted for 'site-responsive' as the term that best describes our examples, except where the artists themselves have used different terminology.

[22] For extended discussions on ANU, Beckett, and the non-place, see Singleton (2013, 2016a, 2016b); for the political significance of ANU's *Laundry*, see Haughton (2014). Augé defines non-place as follows: 'If a place can be defined as relational, historical and concerned with identity, then a space which cannot be defined as relational, or historical, or concerned with identity will be a non-place' (1997, 63).

It was in this post-recession context that the Beckett in the City series, inaugurated in 2009 by Company SJ under the direction of Sarah Jane Scaife, highlighted a political strand in Beckett by placing his work within the canvas of contemporary Dublin. Scaife had a great deal of Beckett experience to draw on: she had directed seven shorts by Beckett at the Abbey Theatre (1989–90), had led the Beckett in Asia project (2000–6) that brought her to seven countries to workshop and direct his plays with non-Irish collaborators, and has adapted *Company* twice (1990 and 2018). Scaife is also a scholar who wrote her PhD, entitled 'The Culturally Inscribed Body and Spaces of Performance in Samuel Beckett's Theatre' (2013), at the University of Reading, and she has published multiple times on the origins and implications of the Beckett in the City project (2016, 154–67; 2018). She describes her aim explicitly in both spatial and political terms: 'My approach to staging Beckett has increasingly focused on the site of each production and its geographical and historical contexts in order to frame continuing experiences of marginalisation that are articulated by Beckett's subjects' (2018, 125–6). Discussing the first piece of the cycle, *Act Without Words II* (2009), Brian Singleton brings out the economic specificities of the period:

> the actors' lean bodies and their physical mime of everyday awakening into reality become charged with social meaning. Inscribed onto these bodies simply through the non-place of the alleyway are the connotations of the leanness of the environment: homelessness, addiction and ill-health. (2016a, 177)

One of the elements that clearly marks this work as experimental is its iterative character. Due to revival opportunities (2010, 2013, and 2014) and touring, the play had to be site-*responsive* rather than site-*specific*. While the text, core principles, and cast remained the same, the place changed, allowing it to be the independent variable. Scaife outlines her principles in seeking appropriate spaces: 'I assessed sites in terms of what they could offer from the chorography of space, time, social, historical and financial signifiers' (2016, 163).[23] The reception of the 2013 version, co-programmed with a new *Rough for Theatre I* and a visual art installation and based in a car park adjacent to the River Liffey, confirmed the legibility of this environment. Reviewing the piece in the *Irish Times*, Fintan O'Toole held that Scaife's use of such places addressed 'one of the crucial dilemmas with contemporary Beckett productions … context' (2013). He invoked a *via negativa* not far removed from Gontarski's caution against filling the void:

---

[23] Scaife adopts the term 'chorography' from a coinage by Mike Pearson in his book *Site-Specific Performance*: 'distinguish[ing] and espous[ing] the unique character of individual places [2010, 31]' (2016, 158).

Beckett's plays have contexts: the second World War and the Holocaust, the threat of nuclear apocalypse, enslavement and oppression, real, observed human miseries. But their aesthetic depends on those contexts remaining almost entirely unstated. They work negatively: we apprehend them because they are almost (but, crucially, not completely) absent. Hence the challenge: leave out the contexts and the plays are arid. Put them in and the plays' immense tact is overwhelmed and reduced to crude pieties. The question Scaife asks is: what if we use place to provide the context? What if the physical setting defines the politics of the piece? The answer is that something very interesting happens then: the plays can function almost purely on an aesthetic level. They don't need to be loaded with too much external meaning precisely because *the place itself does that heavy lifting.* (O'Toole 2013, emphasis added)

The 'heaviness of the lift' being done by a place is increased the more 'marked' the space is, so in Scaife's interior work composed as part of *Beckett in the City* – namely *Fizzles* (2014) in 14 Henrietta Street (a former tenement) and *The Women Speak* in the Halla Banba/Coláiste Mhuire on Parnell Square – there is an even greater focus on the power of the embodied traces arising in and from a *specific* place, redolent of the palpable traces of key moments in local history.[24] As O'Toole points out, without adequate craft such contexts can easily overwhelm; Company SJ's intense focus on the integrity of physical gesture and the specificity of the design and technical choices combine textual and spatial affordances to release new meanings within both. The feet of performers and audience members together on the creaking floors seem to release the memory in the walls, but this is not a gesture of 'reclaiming' a national Beckett; rather, it situates Beckett's *fundamental* human insights in a delicate encounter between living and dead witnesses. It is interesting that when the pieces were installed in a piano factory in Hell's Kitchen in New York (2017), their resonance was not lost; as Scaife points out, many working-class Irish immigrants had once settled in that district (2018, 126). The mobility of such deeply Irish site-responsive work is testament to the regrettable fact that one does not have to scratch the surface of any city very deeply to find traces of the 'too-long-suppressed experience of vulnerable women within such institutional spaces', or 'the legacies of state control over women's spaces and bodies', or 'the disenfranchised of our society' (2018, 126).

Gare St Lazare Ireland's *How It Is (Part One)* (2018) returns to the space of the theatre, but it estranges the mode of audience engagement within that

---

[24] *The Women Speak* included versions of *Not I*, *Footfalls*, *Come and Go*, and *Rockaby*. Both this series and *Fizzles* are explored in greater detail in the next section for their use of sound, light, and video technologies. For a discussion of Halla Banba/Coláiste Mhuire and the significance of her journey with the site, see Scaife (2018, 119–21).

environment so thoroughly that it qualifies as site-responsive. Developed for the Everyman Palace Theatre in Cork, a restored jewel of late Victorian theatrical architecture that originally opened in 1897, the piece transferred to the Print Room at the Coronet in London, a venue of the same era (built 1898).[25] It is the first piece in a cycle of three parts, through which the company intends eventually to perform the entire novel. Developed over multiple years, with a range of partners and residencies including the Centre Culturel Irlandais in Paris, more than one university, and the Everyman Palace Theatre itself, *How It Is* draws on the company's expertise at performing Beckett's prose, an extensive international profile built up by director Judy Hegarty-Lovett and performer Conor Lovett since 1996.

Emerging from experimental and interdisciplinary traditions in their own training and collaborative experiences in both Ireland and France, the company has consistently displayed an embodied sensitivity to both place and audience in all their Beckett work.[26] *How It Is* creates a participatory experience for the audience, in which it enters from the lobby through an artist's entrance, steps through the backstage area past working technicians, and finds itself on the stage of the Everyman behind a red velvet curtain (and a metal safety curtain at half-height). Ostensibly before the show has begun, the members of the creative team introduce themselves; this moment of exposing the inner workings of the theatre, reinforcing the gesture of having revealed the backstage areas to the audience, aligns the work with both modernist and more 'postdramatic' tradi-tions of foregrounding the mechanism and materiality of the theatre. This performance of the novel, multivocal and aleatory as it is, does not seek a figurative rendition of the narrator face down in the mud; instead, like the work discussed elsewhere in this section, it seeks only to cultivate a listening chamber, to bend the communal ear, to prepare an audience to receive a living thought. Hegarty-Lovett has stated that the piece sought to put the audience in the same position as the reader; in an echo of *Not I*, such a gesture stages the *reader's* experience as an *auditor's* experience. This provocative gesture, sus-pended dialectically between faithful presentation of the work's origin and radical re-embodiment of the work's presence, continues the theatrical experi-mentation of the novel itself: 'I say it as I hear it.'

---

[25] For a discussion of the history of the Everyman, see Daly (2017).

[26] A strand of the company's Irish performance history in the mid-2000s, a cycle called 'Access All Beckett', featured non-theatre venues prominently, with performances in Dublin at the National Gallery (*Enough*), and in Cork at the Masonic Temple (*Texts for Nothing*) and Public Museum (*Worstward Ho*). Their frequent reliance on a solo performer created greater flexibility in this regard, with pieces transferring fluidly between theatrical and non-theatrical venues. *How It Is (Part One)* is significantly more site-specific, as currently constructed.

Avant-garde practices of the late twentieth-century theatre, called a 'theatre of images' by Bonnie Marranca (1977), created circumstances in which space itself – especially elaborate set and lighting designs within theatres – can suggest a different starting point than the source text alone. Robert Wilson, discussing how he began work on *Krapp's Last Tape*, is explicit about this priority: 'I start with: what does the stage look like? . . . Once I know what the space looks like, it's much easier for me to decide what to do' (2014, 103). Hegarty-Lovett, who has articulated Gare St Lazare Ireland's *How It Is* as a 'spatial reimagining' of the novel, joins this tradition but revises it in key ways, considering the Everyman – where the company also rehearsed – to be an 'open laboratory'.[27] 'Stage' and 'space' are collapsed into one. 'What does the stage look like?' becomes a radical, expansive, almost existential question in this performance. Wilson's choice of subject and verb – 'me to decide' – echoes Hamm a bit, and signals a less process-oriented model than Gare St Lazare's sustained engagement with collaborators would imply (in this production, actors Conor Lovett and Stephen Dillane, and sound designer/composer Mel Mercier, whose contribution is discussed in greater detail in the next section). Through a deep sensitivity to the space and its echoes, there are 'discoveries' that precede directorial 'decisions', elements that arise both from moments of chance and moments of work, visible and audible manifestations of the novel's voice. *How It Is* shows that site-specificity (in Cork) and site-responsiveness (in London) can retain an experimental character, even within the confines of a theatre, by *really seeing* what the theatre can offer.

Transforming Place: Intermedial Environments

In our final example of experimental Beckettian spaces, we turn to recent 'intermedial' activities in which both the link to the source material and the specificity of embodiment become attenuated, yet the experience of the work is no less intense. If anything, the installations we discuss provide another example of how resonant a strategic void can be: just as intersemiotic translation offers the potency of a 'free' Beckett becoming embedded in a body, so too do intermedial environments extend the radical ambiguity and multiplicity of place in Beckett. This flow between place and Beckett is reciprocal, altering how Beckett's texts are received while at the same time transforming the spaces themselves.

A key thinker of intermediality and Beckett is David Houston Jones, whose richly interdisciplinary exploration in his book *Installation Art and the*

---

[27] Like Scaife, Hegarty-Lovett articulates her practice publicly and speaks in the scholarly community; in 2018 she curated a symposium on *How It Is* in Paris and contributed invited talks to Beckett conferences in both Mexico and Reading. Both of these direct quotations are from her talk at 'Transdisciplinary Beckett' in Mexico, 9 November 2018, available online here: www.youtube.com/watch?v=nft5Q6MMWfA (accessed 3 March 2020).

Practices of Archivalism (2016) opens with the examples of Atom Egoyan's *Steenbeckett* (2002, installed in Enniskillen in 2012) and the Tate Modern Turbine Hall installation *How It Is* by Mirosław Bałka (2009–10). Egoyan, a Canadian filmmaker who directed John Hurt in *Krapp's Last Tape* for the *Beckett on Film* project in 2001, was originally commissioned by Artangel and the former Museum of Mankind in London. In the original installation (recalling the backstage exposure of the Everyman in Gare St Lazare Ireland's *How It Is*), the audience went through a labyrinth of stairs and corridors to a projection booth, where they watched through the viewing window as the final reel of Egoyan's film adaptation – more than 600 metres of 35 mm film, webbed across the walls and floor and ceiling – was continuously run through a Steenbeck flatbed film editor. Overwhelming the senses with the clatter and rattle of the wheels, the installation slowly rendered the reel unusable, gradually washing out the small projection (editors, though not as harsh as film projectors, slowly degrade film). In an adjacent space, the digitally remastered final cut of the same film played in high-definition, unchanging through the duration of the exhibit. By itself, the installation is an astute commentary on the relation between analogue and digital culture, using the machinery and materials of *Krapp's Last Tape* to reflect on the nature of memory and cultural preservation. Critics read the tone as sombre; as Krapp's tape offers a 'farewell to love', Jonathan Jones proposed that *Steenbeckett* says 'goodbye to cinema' (2002).

The installation functioned differently, however, and gained a further layer when sited in the Enniskillen Happy Days Festival (2012). First, it was installed in a gallery space rather than a cinema, without the original labyrinthine and layered quality of journey. Instead of the venue lending weight through architecture, however, what Trish McTighe calls the 'place-archive' spoke back to the work (2018, 34). Houston Jones 'refers to installations which take place in the archive, which appear to appropriate personal archives and which incorporate archival techniques and practices' (2016, 4), and links Beckett to archivalism via the notion of *lieux de mémoire* (see Nora 1989). This aligns well with McTighe's argument for festivals, especially focusing on Enniskillen in the Irish context.

> Places and archival documents are material entities whose only distinction might lie, therefore, in their differential rate of decay. In one sense, place is what happens beyond the limits of the archive, if the archive stands for pieces of the world whose natural pace of decay is interrupted and slowed by curation and preservation. (2018, 34)

McTighe sees the place-archive of Enniskillen operating in two different frames of time, one geological, visible in the strata and lakes and caves, and one historical: the scars of 'plantation, partition, and conflict' (2018, 33). That the gallery hosting *Steenbeckett* was the Clinton Centre, dedicated following the 1998 Good Friday peace agreement on the site of the Remembrance Sunday attack on 8 November 1987, one of the single worst atrocities committed by the IRA (killing twelve and injuring sixty-three), brought a new weight to the meaning of 'remembrance', initiating an expanded reading of both *Krapp's Last Tape* and the environment.

Mirosław Bałka is an internationally celebrated artist based in Poland, where he leads the 'Studio of Spatial Activities' in Warsaw, which he refers to as a 'laboratory' for young artists. In the early 1990s he converted his family home in Otwock, a small town 24 kilometres south-east of the capital where his father worked as a tombstone engraver, into a studio and venue for artistic events. Describing this place as a 'project', Bałka's website states:

> In his practice the artist frequently draws on the memory of the place which changed its original function, its dimensions, its geographic coordinates. Cast models of the house's walls and floors become sculptures. Materials found on site, such as wood, linoleum or ash, continue to exist in Bałka's works. Over recent years, the studio has gradually lost its function, ceasing to be a working space. The 'Otwock' project does not tend to historicize it. Rather, it seeks to explore the potential of the studio as a place of artistic practice and a point of reference. Its future remains open.

Bałka's work is notable first for the degree to which it involves the process of human embodiment as it relates to space. He frequently uses his own embodied measurements as the source for sculptural configurations, or uses the dimensions of the resulting works as their title. In interviews, Bałka refers to the proximity of the former Jewish ghetto to both studios where he has worked (Warsaw and Otwock), and his artworks are frequently haunted by past atrocities, above all the Shoah: his installation *Winterreise (Bambi, Bambi, Pond)* (2003) included deer filmed at Birkenau, *Neither* (2004) featured sculptural variations on the 'Himmelstrasse' to the gas chambers, and his short film *Apple* (2009) was shot on the grounds of Treblinka. Nonetheless, like Beckett and many of the experimental artists referred to so far, Bałka resists the reduction of his work to the one category of 'Holocaust art', often concealing the location of his source material: 'The full name Treblinka is never mentioned specifically, because that would narrow the extensive field of considerations to be explored ... the enigmatic title of the exhibition – *Nothere* – brought to the fore the indeterminateness of place: there and not there simultaneously' (Rottenberg 2017, 42). Interviewing him prior to the Tate installation, Adrian Searle quotes Bałka regarding his work: 'It is about being' (Tate Modern 2009).

How It Is in the Tate Modern was the tenth commission of the Unilever Series, which presents major public, free, and often participatory works of art in the main entrance of the Tate Modern on London's South Bank. Bałka's installation, open from 13 October 2009 to 5 April 2010, is described by the museum:

> a giant grey steel structure with a vast dark chamber, which in construction reflects the surrounding architecture – almost as if the interior space of the Turbine Hall has been turned inside out. Hovering somewhere between sculpture and architecture, on 2-metre stilts, it stands 13 metres high and 30 metres long. Visitors can walk underneath it, listening to the echoing sound of footsteps on steel, or enter via a ramp into a pitch black interior, creating a sense of unease. (Tate Modern 2009)

Given that the experience involves walking up a ramp into pitch darkness, the resonance of sharing a dark space in public with other bodies – perhaps invoking the Holocaust as well as more recent flows of refugees, migrants, and victims of human trafficking – the curators acknowledge that the experience could be 'both personal and collective ... perhaps provoking feelings of apprehension, excitement or intrigue' (Tate Modern 2009). The layering of a Continental European history within the site of contemporary London, together with the weight of cultural capital and postcolonial history implied by the names 'Tate' and 'Unilever' attached to the artwork, reflects something at once more challenging and more mobile than an apparently 'static' artwork may imply. This suggests that Beckettian space is not so much a fixed location as a 'path', to draw on the work of Tim Ingold for its resonance with the novel *How It Is* as well as Beckett's later 'closed space' prose works: 'bound together by the itineraries of their inhabitants, places exist not in spaces but as nodes in a matrix of movement' (2000, 219).

The complex, entangled performances of European identity taking place through and with Beckett and Bałka return us to the notion of what is audience-responsive and what is site-responsive, revealing how much it matters both *where* and *how* Beckett is performed. In the theatrical encounters within Beckettian spaces described in this section, the 'invisible network' of the audience is constitutive: none of the works mentioned so far can function as theatre without that audience. Installation, by contrast, can be more embracing of the non-human transformation of spaces, and by its nature it relinquishes a great deal more control over the individual experience. Nonetheless, even more intense and personal experiences are achievable through the imbrication of materials and contexts, with the embodied responses they evoke. The extension of work like Bałka's into virtual space, with embodied experiences mediated by technology, opens a new set of concerns regarding experimental Beckett in the space of technology, which we take up in the next section.

4 Media and Technology ('First both')

Since the 1990s, we have seen readers, audiences, students, artists, and scholars access Beckett's thought through media that did not exist in Beckett's lifetime, and even the technologies that did exist for him have now changed into something qualitatively different. In this section, we trace some aspects of projects that have responded specifically to the affordances of new media and updated technologies both inside and outside the theatre, in order to establish a trajectory towards possible digital and virtual futures. Observing the experimental possibilities discussed thus far in relation to bodies and spaces, it is noticeable that technological affordances are even now altering both the human relation to embodiment and to environment. Technology thus presents the final 'node' of practice where these epochal changes converge. What can we observe about how technology has changed Beckett in performance to date? What are the performance cultures associated with digital culture? What we can expect from the technologies that are only emerging now, and what might new media come to mean to the Beckett of the future?

Beckett's own use of technology and engagement across media provide a useful guide to what might be conceptually at stake for the 'performing subject in the space of technology' (Causey 2006) or the 'techno-performative subject' of today (Causey and Walsh 2013). To start with, there are no Beckett works that are not dependent for their reception on some form of technology or media. Without advanced digital storage and retrieval systems, the print *oeuvre* would cease to be widely accessible; with the works for theatre, while actors can preserve a limited amount of text in embodied memories and perform outdoors, the requisites for staging a play indoors invariably require systems of some kind, most commonly lighting and sound. Beckett uses technology as a generator of drama within texts: in *Krapp's Last Tape* and *Ghost Trio*, recording/playback audio devices feature prominently as the 'companion' to a solitary figure in the *mise en scène*, in which the devices are physically embraced. Beckett reflects philosophically on the nature of media: across Beckett's prose works, theatre plays, radio plays, film script, and television plays are multiple examples of philosophical reflections *on the medium itself*; titles like *Play* and *Film* signal that a self-aware exploration of form is unfolding within the content. As Beckett grew into radio after 1957, directing after 1966, and an increased pace of writing for television in the 1970s, he increasingly countenanced translations between media, and often was involved in licensing, advising, and occasionally directing his work across different technologically mediated vocabularies.[28] All in all, Beckett worked in every available mass media of his lifetime, all five of which expanded massively during the twentieth century: print, recordings, cinema, radio, and television. We argue that this breadth in his creative acts, encompassing the major changes in the development of human communication that his era underwent, is a key reason for his sustained and still-evolving legacy.

Three additional mass media have come into being since Beckett's death: the Internet, mobile telecommunications, and augmented reality (AR).[29] These have each disrupted the ecosystems of production and technologies of reception of the previous five, enabling newer access routes to the same basic content: tablets or e-readers, online music sharing, streaming services, and podcasting are all growing in market share. To determine what is to be done with Beckett in these new or revised mass media, history may be a guide, since many writers of the past had no access to similar tools in their own era, but their thought or work has nonetheless migrated into the present and fluidly circulated among the currently available media. Looking at writers like Shakespeare or Austen, who are household names mainly because their works were repeatedly digitised, staged, filmed, recorded, serialised, and broadcast during the twentieth century (sometimes at great cost to the source text), the medium's message seems to be: adapt or perish. And here, as anyone who has attended a Beckett post-show discussion in the Anglosphere will know, is a Beckett-specific difficulty.

As addressed in our introduction, it unfortunately remains a dominant perception that Beckett resisted the modification of his stage directions that is automatically required for the adaptation of his work across media. At the same time, among scholars of Beckett, it is also known that his apparent reluctance to transgress what Beckett called 'genre' was, at best, inconsistently applied: Beckett both authorised and collaborated with such translations from stage to screen, including *Waiting for Godot* (first in 1961, then 1977), *Play* (1966), *Not*

---

[28] Each medium mentioned in this section has its own extensive literature within Beckett studies, so this short list of sources offers selected and recent contributions only. For an introductory essay to Beckett's works for radio and screen, see Frost (2009). For radio plays, see Verhulst (2015), Addyman, Feldman, and Tonning (2017), and Beloborodova and Verhulst (2018). For film and television, see Herren (2007), Bignell (2009), and Paraskeva (2017). The year 2018 saw three international conferences that addressed this section's topic area in detail, with future publications anticipated: Beckett and Media (Basel), Beckett and Technology (Prague), and Transdisciplinary Beckett (Mexico City).

[29] 'Augmented reality' refers to visual interfaces that place digital objects within real-world spaces, with both simultaneously perceived by the viewer. The global market size of this technology exceeded USD 1 billion in 2016; a meteoric rise to a market size of USD 170 billion by 2022 is predicted (Consultancy.UK, 2018). The possible applications of such a medium beyond the entertainment sector are extensive, and the technology is now enabled as standard on most recent smartphones, driving much of this predicted growth.

I (1977), and *What Where* (1985), as well as multiple stagings of the radio plays *All That Fall* and *Embers* during his lifetime, and a prodigious quantity of recorded, broadcast, and stage-adapted prose. In our view, this qualifies Beckett as an experimental artist in relation to his texts and their relationship to media. The citation trotted out in nearly every case where a theoretical prohibition on such transmission is mentioned is a letter that Beckett wrote to his publisher Barney Rossett on 27 August 1957, which refers specifically to *All That Fall*. Given its centrality in this discourse and the fact that it is frequently taken out of context, it is quoted at length in what follows:

> *All That Fall* is a specifically radio play, or rather radio text, for voices, not bodies. I have already refused to have it 'staged' and I cannot think of it in such terms. A perfectly straight reading before an audience seems to me just barely legitimate, though even on this score I have my doubts. But I am absolutely opposed to any form of adaptation with a view to its conversion into 'theatre'. It is no more theatre than *End-Game* [*sic*] is radio and to 'act' it is to kill it . . . now for my sins I have to go on and say that I can't agree with the idea of *Act Without Words* as a film. It is not a film, not conceived in terms of cinema. If we can't keep our genres more or less distinct, or extricate them from the confusion that has them where they are, we might as well go home and lie down. (2014, 63–4)

One context that should displace this letter's singular authority is simply temporal: Beckett was fifty-one years old, at which age he had tasted approximately five years of critical success as the author of *Waiting for Godot*, following a previous twenty-five years of relative obscurity and critical failure. After this letter, he would go on to thirty more years of prolific, multi-genre, and intermedial creativity and fame, during which he would learn the craft of directing and repeatedly license exactly the sort of experiments he had rejected here.[30] In the extensive correspondence between Beckett and Alan Schneider in *No Author Better Served*, a collection of letters that detail Beckett's negotiations with the affordances and challenges of putting his work into the world, and which frequently refer to adaptations, August 1957 falls on page 15 of 473 (Harmon 1998); holding to this epistle as though it were the whole gospel grants it undue weight (see Johnson 2016). A second detail that has perhaps been

---

[30] The extent of Beckett's 'craft' as a director is worthy of further commentary that cannot be undertaken in full here (see Knowlson 1987; McMullan 1994). Our position is that directing is clearly important to Beckett's development and to the archive of modernist theatre, but the fact that Beckett's sole credits are for his own work (with the debatable exception of Robert Pinget) renders him an unusual director when considered within performance cultures. Peter Hall, writing in his diary of Beckett's visits to the rehearsal room during his 1974 *Happy Days*, notes: 'Unlike Harold [Pinter], he is not finally a *theatre worker*, great director though he can be. He confuses the work process with the result' (2000, 138, emphasis added).

overlooked in the letter is Beckett's idiosyncratic use of punctuation. He uses 'scare quotes' around the terms 'staged', 'theatre', and 'act', suggesting a tone in which Beckett is referring not to these concepts in general, but rather specifically to a particular approach to staging, acting, and theatre – almost certainly the type of naturalistic theatre in which he went on to intervene so decisively and the type of emotive acting that he cautioned numerous performers against.

Others have examined this letter in detail and found related oscillations that call its primacy into question. Everett Frost has argued convincingly, both in his preface to the new Faber edition that collects the broadcast work and in other contexts, that Beckett's attention to the ontology of the form of broadcast media in which he was writing is what his objections were about. Of concern was the relationship to ambiguity that was essential to the radio work due to its being constituted by voice only, with bodies absent. Regarding *adaphatrôce*, Beckett's pun for the crossing of genre in this way, Frost writes:

> The issue was not primarily about whether or not one might achieve an aesthetically satisfactory result by adapting the work for another medium, but rather of not obliterating its medium-specific intentionalities ... for example, by moving elusively abstract works in the direction of a plausible realism and intelligibility. (2009, xx).

Though Frost expresses scepticism of such projects on the grounds of the first half of this quote, the second half clearly has a loophole. If a theatrical rendering of the radio work could preserve 'elusive abstraction' or avoid 'plausible realism' or even 'intelligibility', then it might not run afoul of such a prohibition. Thus, the notion of a constitutive and productive void in Beckett returns: if ambiguity can still be protected, then *adaphatrôce* might succeed.

Even Beckett himself, in a comment to Ludovic Janvier cited by Frost, shows the same divide, and reveals a surprisingly limited view of what constitutes stage performance. '*Embers* depends upon an ambiguity: does the protagonist have a hallucination or is he in the presence of reality? A visual production would destroy the ambiguity' (2009: ix). Again, one cannot dispute the first half: *Embers* does depend upon an ambiguity. But why is it necessary that visuals destroy ambiguity? Isn't Beckett himself the master of ambiguous visuals? What if a director and designer are interested in how to stage ambiguity, and have worked over decades to hone that skill? It is here that Beckett, and scholars whose ethics are strongly oriented to authorial fidelity, perhaps inadvertently overlook the full impact of modernism, to say nothing of postmodern dramaturgy. The twentieth-century artistic tradition, preceding these comments by fifty years or more, is in many ways an excavation of the idea of ambiguity, a refutation of verisimilitude, and the substitution of the apparent truth of what is *visible* for deeper truths: the dynamic technological realm, for the Futurists; the territory of dreams, for the Symbolists; the realm of emotion, for the Expressionists; the realm of imagination, Eros, and danger, for the Surrealists; the list could go on. Beckett's own insights into ambiguous embodiment and place, his contribution to the theatre, construct a key waystation on the journey towards a postmodern dramaturgy of contemporary politics and thought.

The logic arising from this chain, then, is simple: if we want Beckett to go on being received into the future, a certain degree of adjustment for changing media and new technologies is an inevitability. As we argue later, following both Bernard Stiegler (1998, 2014) and Matthew Causey (2006), such alterations do not need to be inserted proactively, since they are already embedded within the human subject: technologies, especially contemporary affordances like the near-ubiquitous mobile phone, are not sufficiently separate or distinct from humans to evolve separately. Technologically motivated adjustments to Beckett's original texts, rather than being inherently condemned, should thus be considered in light of their impact on constitutive ambiguities. The 'losses' or 'gains' in relation to the original source are not only there when crossing into new media; they are always there in the source media as well, and Beckett already felt acutely their compromises and inconsistencies in his own time and in his 'home' media. These instabilities and innovations that are part of living work are the subject of the next section, which looks first at the impact of new theatre technologies on recent experimental Beckett practices.

Inside the Theatre: Light and Sound

We begin this exploration in the theatre, where Beckett's work remains a key reference for twentieth-century innovations in scenography, and where his texts are widely known for being demanding material from a design and technical perspective. Beckett's extensive record of correspondence with directors, not to mention his personal notations and diagrams gathered in the *Theatrical Notebooks* and sometimes published with the plays, reveal a degree of attention to technical matters of lighting and sound that is not universally associated with playwriting. However, it would be erroneous to think of this merely as a matter of aesthetic control being asserted due to Beckett's visual preferences; rather, the technical features of Beckett's plays are frequently constitutive of the event. In this, Beckett's work is ahead of its time: the turn in theatre and performance scholarship to an expanded view of scenography in terms of 'agency' of the non-human elements such as light, sound, video, or visible objects is a comparatively recent phenomenon.[31]

In relation to lighting specifically, Beckett's plays index a historical transition in which light in performance, initially analysed as a supportive element in service to texts, performers, and spectacle – essentially a utility, like the electricity that enabled it – becomes instead 'structural, constructive, poetic, and dramaturgic' (Crisafulli 2013, 18). *Play* (1963) is recruited as a central example in these discussions, since it is obviously a case where the light itself is the highest-status 'performer' in a scene with three actors reduced to heads only, placed side by side in urns. The light, named 'Sam' by Alan Schneider in the American premiere (Schneider and Schechner 1965, 130), is a fourth player, a 'unique inquisitor' (Beckett 2006, 318), and an ontological necessity for the play to come into being. This renders it a 'creative light' (Palmer 2013) or 'scenographic light' that is 'creative rather than responsive' (Graham 2016, 74), a technological feature that is not merely technical. Beckett's sensitivity about the lighting placement illustrates the point: he diagrammed three alternatives in his *Theatrical Notebooks*, specifying a single source (or at least the impression of a single source) rather than three individual spots, which would have been substantially easier to control (Beckett 1999, 189). Aside from correctly executing more than two hundred lighting cues (if the 'da capo' is included), creating the impression of a single interrogator using an analogue lighting system or a manually operated follow-spot is a challenge, given Beckett's use of 'chorus' moments when all three heads need to be lit together. Precisely how the authority of an 'interrogator' light will be read by the audience is also highly dependent on theatre architecture and directorial choice: if a prompter's box is present and a technician can be concealed with a light, this will achieve a different result from a mounted follow-spot behind the audience or the 'Kabuki' solution of a black-clad co-performer sitting in the front row with the audience, which is different again from three 'locked-off' instruments that appear to be coming from a single location, but obviously could not be a single source.

Digital control over stage lighting, dating from approximately 1986 and now standard across the Anglophone theatre, has enabled an enormously expanded

---

[31] This section is indebted to both the practice and scholarship of designer/scholar Katherine Graham, whose PhD 'Scenographic Light: Towards an Understanding of Expressive Light in Performance' (2018b) was a valuable resource. Both McMullan (2016) and Graham (2018a, 2018b) point out the growing interest in connecting scenography to dramaturgy, as well as the centrality of 'technical' elements of performance in contributing new knowledge to theatre scholarship. Recent surveys of 'expanded' scenography include McKinney and Palmer (2017) and Hann (2018). Graham notes the special issue 'On Scenography' of *Performance Research* (2013) and the launch of the *Journal of Theatre and Performance Design* (2015) as examples of this pivot in the field.

range of complex behaviours and interactions across multiple lighting instruments, compared to the period in which Beckett wrote *Play*.[32] It has also enhanced the technological affordances of single lamps: the availability of 'moving-head' lights with motorised, remote-controlled pan-tilt-zoom functions means that directors can now enact Beckett's vision for *Play* more faithfully and more flexibly, using a single interrogator light moving without a concealed human operator. The shift from analogue to digital lighting has amounted to a significant transfer of creative power to the lighting designer, and should be thought of as a parallel development to the increased dramaturgical agency of scenography more broadly.

The range of possibilities contemporary lighting design offers is, following Causey (2006), already 'embedded' in contemporary theatre and assumed by most practitioners to be an integral part of a theatre process: thus, these new technologies appear in all the recent productions mentioned so far. They are especially foregrounded in the work of designer Aedín Cosgrove, who leads Pan Pan Theatre with Gavin Quinn, and who designed lighting for their three Beckett radio plays (*All That Fall* in 2011, *Embers* in 2013, and *Cascando* in 2016) as well as *Quad* (2014). Quinn is fond of saying that radio is a visual medium (Barry 2016); lighting a radio play for the stage nonetheless involves an intermedial reimagining, highlighting a tension between light and darkness (following Mirosław Bałka, various qualities of darkness are a potent tool in the designer's arsenal). Cosgrove notes that her process involves the reading of Beckett's texts for explicit clues, but she also speaks of entering 'the mind space' of the plays (Crawley 2016), a phenomenological investigation that precedes and conditions the audience's own encounter with the performance as a 'bodied space' (Garner 1994). Even a brief assessment of the lighting across the three Pan Pan radio plays shows the diversity of tactics serving the core strategic aims, which might be summarised in three points: (1) communicating while preserving the texts' ambiguities, (2) sustaining the engagement of the audience, (3) experimenting with the philosophy of theatre (and possibly also radio).

The curated environments in all three Pan Pan radio adaptations (discussed in the previous section) could equally be considered as 'mind spaces', blending the design of light with the sound world Jimmy Eadie created in order to generate a Beckettian corporeal laboratory. In *All That Fall*, audiences heard the recorded text under a constellation of hundreds of soft blue lights suspended from the ceiling, with one full wall packed with golden lanterns (dozens of 'PAR cans'

---

[32] The year 1986 is the year of the first publication of the Digital Multiplex (DMX) communications protocol for controlling stage lighting, as well as the first purchasable/mass-produced 'moving-head' light, the Coemar Robot (see Cadena 2013).

arranged in a rectangular grid). Over the course of the piece, the wall of light gently glowed, built to form various abstracted shapes, occasionally going dark to reveal the twinkling blue above, and reached peak intensity with an affectively overwhelming burst of light and heat, occurring at moments of heightened sound: 'Crescendo of train whistle approaching' (19) and the final 'Tempest of wind and rain' (32).[33] These peak moments of intensity do not suggest a figurative or real-world alignment; rather, in keeping with a core ambiguity of the play, we could simply be inside a skull (this is hinted at, as a skull is printed on the small cushions on the audience's rocking chairs). Progressing to *Embers*, the metaphor extends: a massive sculpture of a skull (large enough to fit two actors inside and built by Andrew Clancy) was given a central position in the scenography, surrounded by hundreds of tiny speakers suspended from the ceiling (almost a sonic echo of the lighting configurations in *All That Fall*, showing a continuity and ongoing dialogue between elements within Pan Pan's practice). Cosgrove lit the skull with such delicacy that it seemed to change and move before our eyes, encouraging a mode of deep attention that can alter time. With analogue technologies and handmade, hand-operated devices hidden in the gantries to scatter light and create a sensation of movement and shimmer, the skull at times seemed to be underwater, again invoking the central question of the text with a light touch. Finally, in *Cascando* (2016), a maze through which the audience walked slowly as a group but with individual headsets containing the soundscape of the play, the light also had a function related to care and safety, ensuring (when required) that the bodies populating the installation would be gently guided, even unconsciously, towards the light. All three of these designs exploit fundamental human capacities for perception to open new depths of meaning in the play, while at the same time depending on a level of precision and control over multiple layers of interacting stage events that is more achievable in the era of digital theatre technology. Cosgrove's designs draw on these new affordances as well as older fundamentals, to re-enact the 'erosion of the inside-outside dichotomy' and to stage the 'mind-world nexus' that Beloborodova and Verhulst identify as key to Beckett's radio dramas in their original medium (2018, 240).

Some of Beckett's most difficult prose offered similarly fertile ground for Gare St Lazare Ireland, whose 2018 production of *How It Is (Part One)* in the Everyman Palace Theatre in Cork often felt like a love letter to the materiality of the theatre and its technologies of representation, even as it responded to the 'mind-world nexus' of the novel. In addition to the view of theatrical elements

---

[33] For an extended analysis of the lighting of *All That Fall* and the combination of 'atmospheric, architectural, and gestural' moments within the design, see Graham (2018a, 269).

normally hidden from view – backstage, safety curtain, working technicians – moments of 'special effect' including the use of costume and recorded voice to disguise actors as one another, the use of sugar glass to create the appearance (and sound) of breaking glass, and an extraordinary illusion in which the theatre's 'ghost-light' (and an actor seen holding it) seemed to float out into the audience. Initially, these seemed to be 'throwback' technologies, a kind of analogue revenge of the machinery of a Victorian theatre. As the piece progressed, however, the dependence on contemporary theatre technologies mounted, supporting and creating powerful moments. Naming only one of these occasions in relation to light, the use of theatrical haze filling the entire auditorium – a tool only coming into its own at the end of Beckett's life, haze allows light to become visible as it travels through space, not only at the place where the beam arrives – generates one of the most memorable visual textures of the production. A body appears with a 'shadow chorus' of other bodies which, in such a haze, seem to be shades or reflections of themselves, with the audience unable to tell how many are present. This manifestation stages the text's indiscernible, fragmented, and refracted identities, while exploiting the theatre's capacity to haunt (Blau 1964).

Underpinning the multiplicity of selves visually staged in *How It Is* is the multiplicity of voices, a quality of the text heard by director Judy Hegarty-Lovett and channelled by sound designer Mel Mercier, who doubles as a performer, oscillating between 'matrixed' and 'non-matrixed' appearances within the space. The opening gesture of the performance is Mercier hitting play on a small cassette recorder, on which Conor Lovett's voice can be heard speaking the opening lines of the novel. As this small sound is gradually supported with the growing intensity of low-end rumbles coming from the auditorium beyond the apron of the stage, a complex mix of the first device's recording, a second voice over a microphone, and speaker playback of more industrial sounds from various locations overwhelms the senses early on. In one passage that felt like a 'living system' with aleatory characteristics, the audience heard different readings at once from the actors at different positions in the space, acting almost as a goad or prompt for one another. In the post-show discussion following the Cork premiere, Mercier disclosed that he was tentative about adding any sound, especially music, but that he found many inspirations for 'improvised polyphony' with voices and 'found sounds' collected in different locations during the extended development. While such a process could be executed in the era of analogue, it certainly could not be achieved with the same efficiency or precision as digital technologies afford for recording, storing, editing, and mixing sound files. Experimentation with such technologies cultivates an environment that, like Pan Pan's listening chambers, returns our attention to the phenomenology of sound itself, which John Cage describes: 'Urgent, unique, uninformed about history and theory, beyond the imagination, central to a sphere without surface, its becoming is unimpeded, energetically broadcast. There is no escape from its action' (1973, 14). The theatre serves not only as a resonator for the sounds of Beckett's texts, but also as a surface on which the cultural change in the medium itself becomes visible. The disruption spreads to encompass theatre history as well: invoking the Symbolist tradition of synaesthesia, we are asked to 'listen to the light' (Beckett 2009a, 35).

Beyond the Theatre: Video and Internet

Nick Kaye describes 'media space' as implying 'the performance of a kind of palimpsest in which real, virtual, and simulated spaces and events negotiate a writing over, reconfiguration, and translation of each other' (2009, 129). While such translational activity – for example video playback or mediation of live performance – certainly occurs extensively in contemporary theatre spaces as well, this section focuses on three types of non-theatre mediation. First, returning to the work of Company SJ, we assess Beckettian experiments that deploy video within site-specific performance environments. Second, returning to the work of Touretteshero and looking briefly at *The Endgame Project* (2017), we explore the significance of Beckettian digital video for the public entirely outside of a theatre context. Finally, we briefly examine the role of the internet and Beckett in performance, which we believes facilitates not only enhanced educational affordances in accessing Beckett, but also a new frontier of Beckettian experimentation both 'in the wild' (McCarthy 2009, 103) as well as for established scholars and artists. Ulrika Maude could have been writing about the internet when she wrote that 'new technologies change the way in which we see, hear and more generally perceived the world, producing in us a double-perception that differs from earlier modes of perceiving' (Maude 2009, 8). How might we perceive Beckett now in screened and streaming contexts, in the 'palimpsest' of today's media landscape?

Experimental use of video is apparent as a key ongoing strand in the site-specific and site-responsive work of Company SJ. Director Sarah Jane Scaife frequently collaborates with Kilian Waters, a filmmaker and video designer whose production values are firmly rooted within digital culture; the affordances of digital capture, editing, screening, and archiving are as essential to the present ecosystem of video as are current sound and light technologies to the theatre. Scaife and Waters have collaborated on both 'interior' pieces of *Beckett and the City*, *Fizzles* (2014, at 14 Henrietta Street) and *The Women Speak* (2015, at Halla Banba). Scaife says of her process with Waters that

they have 'very clear ideas of what the improvisational and aesthetic para-
meters will be for what we are about to film before we start' (2018, 123). Her
approach is rooted in the environment: 'I am constantly thinking of framing,
so that I can visualize how and where the piece will be projected onto the
walls of the performance site' (2018, 123). Scaife also uses video in her
practice in a way that unifies sound and light through embodiment. Referring
first to *Fizzles*, she writes:

> We foregrounded the performing body (Raymond Keane) and layered the live
> body with projected images (created by Kilian Waters), the recorded voice of
> the actor (with sound artist Tim Martin), and the architecture, light, and space
> of the large, decayed rooms. In 2015, we continued this project by introdu-
> cing women's voices. Using the same tools of the body, sound, site, history,
> movement, architecture, and projection, we made flesh the deeply scarred
> voices of Beckett's women and re-situated them in relation to the city and
> institutions of Ireland's past. (118)

Video content, in Waters and Scaife's deployment, opens a portal to multiplicity
of space and multivalence of meaning. It would not do this by itself, outside of
the context of the environment; it gains its qualities by being placed within the
same room as the live performer(s) and live audience(s), framed within the
architecture but simultaneously introducing an additional location. When the
work travels, as *The Women Speak* did to New York, then the video functions as
another link back to Ireland, bringing a local room with the production. The
mobility and malleability of space and embodiment in the context of video,
especially in the hybrid, installation-type environments illuminated by
Company SJ, point towards one avenue of how video can be used in performance not as a substitution for the live, but rather as a complicating enhance-
ment of the source materials' instabilities, a means to access and multiply the
essential non-alignment of spaces and embodiments.

Though a short video also featured within the Touretteshero *Not I* production
(2017), it led to a sense of consolidation of self and space rather than expansion,
serving a documentary function in relation to the process and implications of
what the audience had just seen. The longer documentary of which it was a part,
entitled *Me, My Mouth and I* (2018), enabled viewers to follow Jess Thom
through the process of bringing *Not I* to the stage.[34] That the documentary was
broadcast on BBC2 and later available online reveals the capacity of digital
video technology to disseminate Beckettian content beyond the space of
a production, extending the aesthetic and embodied properties of the original

---

[34] *Me, My Mouth and I* was transmitted on 21 July 2018, and then available on BBC iPlayer through
August 2018.

texts and ideas into a new space, for audiences to appreciate and engage with the work in a new way. The film will have brought a new online audience to Beckett, especially those interested in disability rights and social inclusion issues. As a result, those viewers may have encountered Beckett for the first time, and due to the rigorous nature of the Touretteshero process, they will have heard Beckett scholars share their deep knowledge of the work with Thom in conversation. The interview with Rosemary Pountney is the most evocative, where she recalls that performing *Not I* 'really is a memory feat' before Thom tells her: 'there's no way I'm not going to be able to tic for thirteen minutes'. Pountney's embodied memory of performing Mouth has been captured here, and is shown in transmission to Thom. What is particularly interesting is the memory of the experience as a 'memory feat' and the neurological challenge this may pose for Thom with regard to her tics. For our study of experimental Beckett in performance, this highlights the increased availability of process-based documentation arising in digital culture, potentially reaching a larger audience than the performance itself.

A comparison with the recent film *The Endgame Project* (2017), document-ing the experience of Dan Moran and Chris Jones – two professional actors both diagnosed with Parkinson's, who collaborate to perform *Endgame* off-Broadway – is apposite here. Writing of the stage version of this *Endgame* in a nuanced article for *JOBS*, Patrick Bixby notes: 'the *Endgame* project pro-mised to draw the attention of the theatre audience to corporeal difference as a nexus of observation and contemplation in the theatre' (2018, 118). But the possibilities for social impact the documentary *The Endgame Project* affords, when screened for medical practitioners, carers, families, or any people living with neurological diseases, are clearly much greater, and with digital archiving and circulation, more able to endure. Besides bringing a new audience to Beckett, such work brings Beckett to new audiences in a different guise, in a way that 'can directly impact social and political views regarding physical and mental difference in a manner that surpasses what me might call the merely literary or artistic' (Bixby 2018, 121).

Finally, we turn to the internet itself, a virtual terrain where Beckett not only is disseminated in both established and experimental modes, but also is inter-preted, adapted, translated, and re-embodied by both transmitters and receivers. The internet represents a sudden and drastic acceleration of what McMullan has called, speaking of Beckett's works for radio and television, 'body-circuits' or 'body-transmitters' (2010, 80), because it is a 'convergent' medium, having consolidated older media in order to achieve dominance. Sean McCarthy argues that Beckett was a 'convergent artist', welcoming 'technology to revivify the older theatrical form while also critiquing the possibility of transcendence through the technology alone' (105). But as we consider the proliferation of Beckettian objects online, it raises profound issues about the nature of legal freedoms and cultural capital in digital environments, many of which remain unresolved – for example, the extended and outsized impact of the entire 2002 *Beckett on Film* project (regardless of quality), merely by virtue of its having been uploaded to YouTube piece by piece, and not apparently representing a significant enough cost to anyone to take down. We can compare empirically what the past ten years of YouTube has meant to this legacy by reviewing McCarthy (2009), where he reports 126 results on the search 'Godot' and 'Beckett' in the year 2008; a search in December 2018 returned 35,300 results. The 'impossible heap' indeed: in this plethora of unlicensed material, how will future readers, students, artists, or scholars find Beckett?

Beckett's experimental entanglement in the online environment has blended the brief and irreverent – videos like 'Waiting for Elmo' (2005) or 'Waiting for Godot: The Video Game' (2010) – with sustained, made-for-internet work that substantially responds to the source text but translates it for the online realm. McCarthy explains the trend: 'Because Beckett's texts thrive in the nowhere spaces of online environments, and because these texts explore the limits of communication itself, they are useful for experiments in the relationship between live performance and online communication' (108). Works he explores in detail include Desktop Theater's waitingforgodot.com (1997), a staging of the play in a chatroom environment created by Adriene Jenik and Lisa Brenneis, and *Eh Joe* (2007), produced in Second Life by a Dutch theatre director, whose avatar was named SaveMe Oh.[35] Since the publication of McCarthy (2009), Second Life has not lived up to its promise – McCarthy foresaw a 'Beckett island' for education and the staging of his plays in the virtual space – but Beckett continues to proliferate freely on the Web.

When J. M. Coetzee published his 1973 article 'Samuel Beckett's *Lessness*: An Exercise in Decomposition' in the journal *Computers and the Humanities*, boundaries between computing and the arts were already being transgressed. A series of digital projects have since explored the endless permutations of Beckett's text, including *Possible Lessnesses* (2000) and *End/Lessness* (2017).[36] The latter, a 'durational-digital "after-life" for [Rosemary] Pountney and Beckett', links Pountney's recordings of the component sentences of *Lessness* to 'the computational model of time to play every permutation of the sentences, without repetition, from 2017 until completion' (Heron 2018). Beckett's endless afterlives online are further evoked by Ken Alba's

---

[35] For an extended discussion on Beckett and gaming, see Bohman-Kalaja (2007).

[36] See Heron (2018) for a full description of the project *End/Lessness*: www.end-lessness.co.uk; see Drew and Haahr (2002) for *Possible Lessnesses*: www.random.org/lessness.

experiments with Twine (an open-source non-linear storytelling tool) to create a Web-based 'fictive object' out of the short prose text *Ceiling* (2018), and Unity (a cross-platform game engine) to develop *Quad* (2018) into a Web-based version called *endlessgame*.[37] Here again we are reminded of the radical openness of Beckett in performance, in both theatrical and digital environments, as digital culture brings forth new translations of his writing in ways that confuse the boundaries between the authorial and the participatory, between the textual and the embodied, and between the (closed) Beckett as misunderstood in the past and the (open) reality of the Beckettian in the future.

Towards the Virtual: Virtual Reality, Augmented Reality, and Artificial Intelligence

Building on the interest in a computational Beckett that began more than forty years ago, the possibility of a human–virtual interface within Beckettian theatre practice dates back more than twenty years, to the work of Lance Gharavi (1996) and David Saltz (1996).[38] The new affordances of advanced visualisation, computation, robotics, and deep learning systems are in the process of integrating with the expanding mass media of virtual reality/ augmented reality (VR/AR) content systems, which will lead to another 'phase-shift' (Simondon 1958) in the production and reception of Beckett's works, akin to what happened with the rise of the internet in the 1990s. One of the few major projects in this nascent area includes Sarah Kenderdine and Jeffrey Shaw's *UNMAKEABLELOVE* (2008), an experience based on the late prose text *The Lost Ones*. The project website describes the piece as:

> a physically immersive three-dimensional space of representation that constitutes an augmentation and amalgamation of real and virtual realities. It is a hybrid location-based manifestation that operates both as an individual and socially shared experience, and its interactive modalities of operation incorporate the kinaesthetic dimensions of human apprehension to establish a congruence of human and machine agency.

Linking the new availability of virtual embodiments and computerised scenography to the strong traditions of Beckettian embodiment and space, particularly the installation, this new form is difficult to classify. Is it an homage to Beckett, a citation, an adaptation, an intersemiotic translation, or an entirely new work? Is

---

[37] See http://especiallygreatliterature.com/endlessgame.html and http://especiallygreatliterature
.com/twineceiling.html to experience these projects.

[38] Gharavi developed *Play* for an early version of VR called i-Glasses, demonstrated in 1996; Saltz created a show at Stony Brook called *Beckett Space: A Modernist Carnival* that featured nine Beckett plays, each with human–technology interfaces playing simultaneously and continuously. See Jaleshgari (1996) for a review.

Beckett acting as a stylistic influence while also providing the source? In the ecological model, is Beckett a stem cell for this work, or a viral vector?

Modes of receiving or rethinking Beckett now exist that were either unavailable or unimagined at the time of the work's genesis, marking an evolutionary shift in the ecology of his work. The next phase of these changes that can be envisioned as an outgrowth of present trends, in the next thirty years, may be even more daunting, involving robotic or cyborg performers, AI directors or designers, or ever-more embedded mobile technologies. Even as AR and VR become more pervasive and universal means of exploring media content, they will also alter and accelerate the ways in which scholarship is conducted. This revolution is already here with digital humanities, and large database projects like the Beckett Digital Manuscript Project (BDMP) and Staging Beckett show its potential, but still greater alterations of how we conduct practice, scholarship, and teaching are likely to arise from continued exploitation of deep learning algorithms, computer-assisted performance, and the expansion of virtual content systems.

Such a future may seem at first to be a daunting one, and indeed anxiety seems to be the dominant affect when society confronts such changes. Generally this anxiety takes the form of a concern about humans being replaced, overtaken, or transformed beyond recognition. We see both theoretical and practical reasons why these fears, at least as they relate to Beckett in performance, may be misplaced. First, the evolution of the human and of the technological are not possible to separate; this is a false binary. Writing in *Contemporary Performance Review* about *Virtual Play* (2017), Johnson and O'Dwyer say the following about VR:

> Drawing on the theories of the posthuman from N. Katherine Hayles (*How We Became Posthuman*, 1999) to Rosi Braidotti (*The Posthuman*, 2013), the evolution of this technology *is* the evolution of the human; any attempt to oppose the two in a false binary is to misunderstand that each is the essence of the other. The human body is a technical body. However, the evolution of technology is taking place at a mind-boggling speed, and it is continually accelerating. The overriding condition that characterises these 'technosomatic' evolutionary surges is that they force a renegotiation of rules: how we think and act, as well as how we make art. (Johnson and O'Dwyer 2018)

This line of reasoning, as well as the term 'technosomatic', is indebted to the thinking of Bernard Stiegler (1998, 2014), who is himself rereading the anthropology of thinkers like André Leroi-Gourhan (1993), who argues for a non-human influence on genetic expression (the epigenetic layer). Stiegler innovates and develops this thought by introducing the term 'epiphylogenesis'[39] to

---

[39] He defines the term as 'that store of memory that is particular to a unique life form – the human . . . It is a matter of memory retained in things' (2014, 33).

discuss how human memory evolves somewhere between object and event, interior and exterior, deeply entwined with – in fact, inextricable from – the evolution of the technological tool.

The projects addressed in this section arise from the phase shift in mass media from analogue to digital technology, exploring the implications for prose, radio, theatre, and television after those media have undergone transformations that make them substantively different from the time that Beckett was writing within them. To those scholars, practitioners, or agents who expect that all artists must continue to keep faith with Beckett's precise methods and specific directions, this dynamic and evolutionary model poses a meaningful challenge: 'the place is the same, but no longer coincides with itself' (Connor 2006, 167).

5 Beckett Beyond Boundaries: A Dialogue

Nicholas Johnson (NJ):   'Total object, complete with missing parts, instead of partial object. Question of degree' (Beckett 1984, 138). In our conversations about how to conclude a project that is intended to leave a great deal still open, I recall that you felt that a philosophical dialogue might be an appropriate solution. Why?

Jonathan Heron (JH):   For me, an academic dialogue is both experimental (in the sense of 'thought experiment') and performative (in that we are still wrestling with these ideas). Methodologically, the form gives both readers and authors the space to reflect upon the sections above and consider how they might read and experience Beckett differently. This form also responds to our content on embodiment, environment, and technology by demonstrating a matrixed approach to the performance cultures under investigation. Given the radical openness of contemporary performance practice on Beckett, I feel that an anti-conclusion – a Beckettian refusal to end – would be more fitting for a relatively brief and necessarily selective survey of experimental embodiments. A dialogue stands in for a final judgement like a witness testimony at a trial, and heightens our *situatedness* in relation to the subject matter.

NJ: When researching the controversies of the 1990s that we started with, I was fascinated to re-read the declarations of theatre critic Michael Billington in the *Guardian*, five years after he used almost identical sentences when writing about the Warner/Shaw *Footfalls* fracas: 'Beckett wrote a handful of durable masterpieces but ... at a certain point, his work acquired a theatrical fixity that denies it classic status ... many of his later works lack the possibility of re-interpretation that is the precondition of a classic' (1999). While not sharing his preoccupation with enumerating 'classics', we can now evaluate that statement in light of the evidence we have presented. What does it show?

JH: My sense is that there is a generational shift here, and I too have resisted the view that these works are somehow doomed as 'museum pieces' forevermore. The writing of Peter Brook in *The Empty Space* on Beckett's 'holy theatre' is problematic in this regard, as it both reinforced the notion of authorial creation, while positioning him within 1960s politics of liberation: 'Beckett at his finest seems to have the power of casting a stage picture, a stage relationship, a stage machine from his most intense experiences that in a flash, inspired, exists, stands there complete in itself, not telling, not dictating, symbolic without symbolism. For Beckett's symbols are powerful just because we cannot quite grasp them: they are not signposts, they are not textbooks nor blueprints – they are literally creations' (Brook 2018, 26). 'Creations' puts us back into the realm of liveness, the metaphor of Beckett's work as his offspring, does it not?

NJ: From dust to dust, that's literature. There is a line I love in Roberto Bolaño's *Amuleto*, when the narrator says, '*que el polvo siempre se ha avenido con la literatura*' (1999, 13) which Chris Andrews rendered as 'dust and literature have always gone together' (2006, 4). In the first moment, questioning this proposition, we think of the physical books and scripts, the objects that sit in our offices and gather dust. Then the first explosion comes: dust is mostly skin cells, mostly ourselves, covering our own books, the result of our embodiment co-existing with literature. But then the second explosion, an existential one: literature is also an embodied *event*, and over the course of geological time, all this literature is born astride a grave, in the process of disappearing, along with all humanity. Yet we write it. And this same bravery appears in Beckett, this same consciousness of an end, of an artistic legacy that has begun immediately to die, and yet strangely and persistently endures.

JH: When I worked with Rosemary Pountney on her reading of *Lessness* (that would become the digital-durational project *End/Lessness*), I was reminded of this notion of literary object as an endless event, even in a post-human context, via the digital. My interest within our study of performance practice is that Beckett seems to be an enduring catalyst, or recurring stimulus, for contemporary artists' experiments with form.

NJ: One thing I'm still wondering is how free those experiments will become, as we approach 1 January 2060 ('public domain day', marked in our calendars). A metaphor frequently used by the Beckett Estate has been that Beckett's works are like musical scores, specifically the late Beethoven string quartets, in which 'interpretation' is not to be restricted, but in which all are based on the same 'notes, tonalities, dynamic and tempo markings' (Beckett 1994). I am reminded of the point that Ian Rickson made to you about the text of *Krapp's Last Tape* as a 'recipe' (2014, 98). In both these cases, there is a kind of primary text, a blueprint of a future moment that will need embodiment, space, technology, and plenty of adjustment before it comes to life. But in this work we have argued that texts are even more organic than that: living beings, like a child or an unruly adolescent, waiting until they turn seventy to attain independence from their creator. What does the metaphor of text as *actually* living afford us?

JH: This metaphor extends to the epigenetic approach to text, as we've outlined, especially the way in which Beckett evolved his work through manuscript drafts and theatrical notebooks. Our interest in his creative process has strongly influenced how we approach research methods, which are seeking to be as inter-disciplinary as his own writing.

NJ: I am noticing how object-focused studies about manuscripts might not take into consideration a performance history as a feature of the progres-sion of the manuscript through time, or the ways in which Beckett's practices as a director or collabora-tor or experimenter in theatre might affect the way that we read it. I am encouraged to see that the BDMP editions seem to be going further, and that those manuscripts also feature the *Theatrical Notebook* revisions, while the BDMP 'making of' monographs try to grapple with issues that arose through the performances.

JH: There is a methodological interdisciplinarity here that blurs the space of literature and theatre, of archive and performance, relating to the case stu-dies in the preceding sections, where we become aware that there are several different types of event being produced from Beckett's objects. These events are interdisciplinary when bodies, sites, and media remain open to evolution within theatrical performance and exposed to multiple trends within contemporary performance. In my view, this extends the experimental legacy of Beckett's work.

NJ: Definitely – but there are still tendencies that will likely keep some Beckettian camps separate in the wild. Even if they begin to share a common voca-bulary and common interests, the skills that advanced theatre practitioners need may be sub-stantively different from, say, manuscript scholars. Most directors in the world will still probably just buy a script that is licensed, and perform it 'as is' (as per the contract), without much over-arching awareness that there are fifteen different versions or oscillations across the different publications that exist. Conversely, if you're a manuscript scholar who is engaged in that work in a deep way, and you're great at reading the handwriting, coding it up in XML, and interpreting its deeper cognitive impulses, this doesn't mean that you understand what it takes to put up a play on stage and why that might matter to you. Being able to read across boundaries in this way is not native to the highly disciplinary way in which we're taught or trained, but it's increasingly important that we do intersect.

JH: It has become increasingly important to entangle, both from a disciplinary viewpoint and a practice-as-research perspective. The words that emerged over our writing about embodiment, environment, and technology all have a spatial complexity and a physical multiplicity: 'network', 'node', and 'matrix' were all reconsidered for how they might describe the forms and practices that we see in this Beckettian ecosystem. It suggests that the evolutionary model will not depend on one strand or lineage of practice, or even the intersection of more than one, but rather on the whole 'tangle' changing gradually through layered interactions over time.

NJ: It certainly appears that Beckett studies is increasingly interdisciplinary, and the dimension of 'applied' Beckett has bearing on what the insights of the twentieth century meant, or go on meaning. Those claims seem defensible, if not quite falsifiable. We also wrote that experiments with Beckett might hold promise for engagement with wider social challenges and transdisciplinary research problems. How can we justify that?

JH: Firstly, an important distinction needs to be made about interdisciplinarity. Are we, in using this phrase, talking about interdisciplinary *artistic* practice, where intersections between modes of practice – whether that be movement or theatre, live art and digital media, or music and dance – become part of how artists (like those covered in the preceding sections) like to approach their work? Interdisciplinarity in the scholarly context implies a disciplinary collaboration between arts and sciences, or between disciplines, for example, neuroscience and the social sciences. We can see that Beckett is already taught in interdisciplinary formations and structures through the curricula of schools, colleges, and universities, where he is used as an example of literature, languages, philosophy, theatre, film and television. Indeed, Beckett within environmental, digital, and medical humanities remains a growth area for interdisciplinary research with his writing. Yet there is a third category which we might call the *transdisciplinary* application of Beckett to non-Beckettian territories. These 'applied Becketts' include practice experiments with his writing in participatory or public environments, such as the street, the prison, or the clinic. This transfusion of aesthetic practice into an ethical domain, towards a specific community or a political purpose, is another experimental entanglement worthy of further study.

NJ: One of the alignments that is implied by the 'applied' or 'political' experimental Beckett is a return to the idea of the Century, by which I mean the twentieth – Beckett's 'long century' (Badiou 2008) – in which he bridges a gap in thinking between aesthetic modernism and postmodern dramaturgy, without quite trusting or belonging to either camp. He doesn't accept unities or offer 'ever-more-faded positivities' (Adorno 1983, 381), but nor is he fully yielding his authority; he hasn't fully signed up to the project of redress. I wonder if in his quest in this long, troubled period of history simply to go on, and to go on witnessing, is part of what sets up this interesting dialectic in performance, between the stricture of the thing we are given, together with the incredibly wide proliferation of meanings. Is the power of the void so explosive as that?

JH:

Disciplines are organizations of power and episte-mic encampments (a phrase that we've used before). The discourse around 'pure' and 'applied' disciplines may be useful here; the idea that one student can have a *purely* aesthetic relationship to literature and philosophy, and another can have *only* an applied relationship to arts and culture, is an unhelpful binary with a troubling ethical dimen-sion. We also have pure and applied mathematics, 'hard' sciences and applied sciences, so there is something here around purity and application which helps us to think about interdisciplinary Becketts as 'pure' and 'applied', or as the literature on interdisciplinarity would have it, as 'critical' and 'instrumental' (Frodeman 2010, 15).

NJ:

Perhaps what we are suggesting is that if we build a wall between the pure and the applied, then we separate theory and practice too much. I think we are positing instead that there is a domain of 'praxis', which is fusing and politicizing the engagement between theories that are practised in space with bodies and time (on the one side) and practices which are heavily theorized (on the other). Praxis is the zone of *flow* where Beckett comes into being, a 'path' rather than a destination (Ingold 2000, 219). Instead of allowing separation to embed, we are tracking praxis into this zone that we are calling 'experimentation', where things min-gle unpredictably. Insights from this terrain of experimental Beckett then alter the structure and dissemination of knowledge, and how we teach or represent Beckett to the next generation will be changed by this approach.

JH:

Exactly – it's clear that these issues are not simply methodological but also pedagogic, and I am inter-ested in how these ideas might inform a critical peda-gogy (cf. Freire 1968) for Beckett studies, in the same way that Boal adapted Freirean praxis to his *Theatre of the Oppressed*. One powerful thing about Beckettian praxis is its relationship to failure, especially the revaluation of failure within artistic and epistemic projects, captured by those lines from *Worstward Ho*: 'Try again. Fail again. Fail better' (2009b, 81). Not only is there a potent experimental value to failure, which I have discussed elsewhere (Heron and Kershaw 2018), but there is also an inherently pedagogic theme of ignorance and un-knowing. Our laboratory work on *Worstward Ho* (2014, Science Gallery Dublin) exploring Beckett's failure in a scientific context helped us to reflect on both interdisciplinarity and intermediality. Our participants noticed that Beckett's failure was being productively but problematically used by the Science Gallery to tell a story about success, under the banner of 'failing better'. We observed that 'failure' for Beckett was not the same as it is for scientists and entrepreneurs. Indeed, there is already a discourse and disciplining of failure within performance practices, such as live art and queer performance (Le Feuvre 2010; Halberstam 2011).

NJ: Central to the question of education and critical pedagogy with Beckett is that of power, and when power is under discussion, the next question is bound to be justice, which is about how power should be allowed to operate (or not). As far as questions of social justice, there is a clear connection in Beckett's biography: he reflexively concerned himself with the protection of the weak, struggles for national determination, opposition to torture, opposition to detention without trial (both physically and metaphysically).

JH: And I wonder how this relates to his compassion, given his preoccupation with vulnerable or marginal figures.

NJ: Yes. There is a question here about whether contemporary life is making some of these Beckettian questions more urgent, and whether experimental Beckett could be a stronger pedagogical tool in this regard. There are still empowered authorities in Beckett: we listed them on our first page. I like the idea that a critical pedagogy, or an experimental practice with Beckett, could support the pursuit of a more *just* outcome for those who engage with education, research, or artistic practice around Beckett. Actor training, for example, is ripe for its Beckettian pedagogical revolution. But then, what constitutes a 'just mode' of working with Beckett certainly is malleable, based on context, and it isn't the same for all people everywhere.

JH: It's negotiated.

NJ: It's negotiated. But the drift seems to be weighted towards openness, if only because of the inevitability of entropy, the final consequences of *going on*. It is interesting to think about projects, in relation to pedagogical implications or effects, being assessed or judged based on the extent to which they contribute to a growing openness of people having and receiving Beckett, or Beckettian insights.

JH: When we talk about the pedagogy of experimental practice, there is a fundamental question about whether the process is open or closed; how does that work in relation to Beckett?

NJ: We have two propositions: the first is that closed experiments with Beckett have a value, and the second is that open experiments do too. We are thinking here about the ongoing definition of the boundaries of aesthetic production that help us to articulate Beckettian performance as an area of cultural investigation. There is an ongoing recreation and renewal of these texts for each generation.

JH: Even though a laboratory is necessarily a closed space for experimentation, it can also be an open process for the systematic exploration of practice, while maintaining a disciplinary rigour of movement, voice, sound, or text.

NJ: I am thinking not just of experimental spaces as closed, but also of the texts themselves as circumscribed, and defining of the sequence of events that needs to happen. And each play text is first, in a sense, a closed experimental space.

JH: Practitioners and performers often remark upon the simultaneous limitation and liberation of the Beckettian text, which resonates with this notion of open and closed experimentation.

NJ: Another area of openness around the Beckettian text is the proliferation of Beckett as a meme through the culture in unpredictable (again) and pervasive ways. Beckettian aesthetics have virally self-propagated to so many different arenas of scholarly and studio practice that it's difficult to trace influence now – so many writers are breathing and living in that terrain, consciously or not. I think it's the first line of Steven Connor's book: 'For many writers, Samuel Beckett becomes a kind of life sentence' (2014, 1). The strands are so numerous, and the derivatives so prolific, that we can't track them all – we've only identified some moments, both in and beyond the theatre, where this is explicit.

JH: A study of the implicit in Beckettian performance would be another avenue here, as so many have taken an image or a fragment as a stimulus and then translated it into a new art form – in code, in art, in dance, and so on –

NJ: If Beckett gave the world a set of texts, systems, and practices that changed the theatre and media of his time, perhaps keeping faith with his avant-garde legacy entails performing disruption: allowing that the engine of evolution – the key to survival of his phylum – is, in fact, mutation. I am told that good parenting involves giving one's offspring both roots and wings. If we are custodians or guardians of a raw youth known as the Beckett *oeuvre*, then perhaps we should be training that work for flexibility over rigidity, movement over stasis, openness to experimentation and tolerance of risk, resilience in the face of inevitable failures and struggles. In short, an experimental and educative ethos can secure for Beckett a sustainable environment where there is still room to grow.

References

Abbott, H. Porter (1996), *Beckett Writing Beckett: The Author in the Autograph* (Ithaca, NY: Cornell University Press).

Abrahami, Natalie (2015), 'An Interview with Natalie Abrahami', with Jonathan Heron, in: *Journal of Beckett Studies*, 24.2: 247–58. DOI:10.3366/jobs.2015.0140

Addyman, David, Matthew Feldman, and Erik Tonning, eds. (2017), *Samuel Beckett and BBC Radio: A Reassessment* (New York: Palgrave Macmillan). DOI:10.1057/978-1-137-54265-6

Adorno, Theodor [1966] (1983), *Negative Dialectics*, trans. by E. B. Ashton (New York and London: Continuum).

Alger, Jonathan (2010), 'Review: "How It Is" from Tate Modern', *MuseumMobile Wiki*, URL: http://wiki.museummobile.info/archives/6658.

Augé, Marc (1997), *Non-places: An Introduction to Supermodernity*, 2nd ed. (London and New York: Verso).

Badiou, Alain (2008), *The Century* (Cambridge: Polity).

Bailes, Sara Jane (2011), *Performance Theatre and the Poetics of Failure* (London and New York: Routledge)

Bailes, Sara Jane and Nicholas Till, eds. (2014), *Beckett and Musicality* (Farnham: Ashgate).

Barad, Karen (2007), *Meeting the Universe Halfway: Quantum Physics and the Entanglement of Matter and Meaning* (Durham, NC: Duke University Press).

Barry, Aoife (2016), 'It's dark, you're sitting on stage in a rocking chair, and a woman's voice booms out … ' *thejournal.ie*, 10 February. URL: www.thejournal.ie/all-that-fall-abbey-theatre-2595951-Feb2016/.

Bateson, Gregory [1972] (2000), *Steps to an Ecology of Mind* (Chicago: University of Chicago Press).

Beckett, Edward (1994), 'The wrong route to the heart of Beckett', *The Guardian* (Letters), 24 March 1994.

Beckett, Samuel [1972] (1984), *Disjecta: Miscellaneous Writings and a Dramatic Fragment*, ed. by Ruby Cohn (New York: Grove).

(1999), *The Theatrical Notebooks of Samuel Beckett, Volume 4: Shorter Plays*, ed. by S. E. Gontarski (New York: Grove).

(2006), *The Complete Dramatic Works* (London: Faber & Faber).

(2009a), *All That Fall and Other Plays for Radio and Screen*, ed. by Everett Frost (London: Faber & Faber).

(2009b), *Company / Ill Seen Ill Said / Worstward Ho / Stirrings Still* (London: Faber & Faber.)

(2010), *The Unnamable* (London: Faber & Faber).

(2014), *The Letters of Samuel Beckett, Volume III, 1957–1965*, ed. by G. Craig, M. Dow Fehsenfeld, D. Gunn, and L. More Overbeck (Cambridge: Cambridge University Press).

Beloborodova, Olga and Pim Verhulst (2018), 'Broadcasting the Mind: Extended Cognition in Beckett's Radio Plays', in: *Beckett and Modernism*, ed. by Olga Beloborodova, Dirk van Hulle, and Pim Verhulst (Cham, Switzerland: Springer), 239–58.

Benedetti, Jean (2008), 'Translator's Foreword' in Stanislavski, pp. xv–xxii.

Ben-Zvi, Linda, ed. (1992), *Women in Beckett: Performance and Critical Perspectives* (Urbana and Chicago: University of Illinois Press).

Bignell, Jonathan (2009), *Beckett on Screen: The Television Plays* (Manchester: Manchester University Press).

Billington, Michael (1999), 'Plays for Today', *The Guardian*, 1 September. URL: www.theguardian.com/culture/1999/sep/01/artsfeatures2

Bixby, Patrick (2018), '"this . . . this . . . thing": The Endgame Project, Corporeal Difference, and the Ethics of Witnessing', in: *Journal of Beckett Studies* 27.1: 112–27. DOI:https://doi.org/10.3366/jobs.2018.0224

Blau, Herbert (1964), *The Impossible Theater: A Manifesto* (New York: Macmillan).

Bohman-Kalaja, Kimberly (2007), *Reading Games: An Aesthetics of Play in Flann O'Brien, Samuel Beckett & Georges Perec* (Champaign, IL: Dalkey Archive).

Bolaño, Roberto (1999), *Amuleto* (Barcelona: Anagrama).

(2006), *Amulet*, trans. by Chris Andrews (New York: New Directions).

Borgdorff, Henk (2012), *The Conflict of the Faculties: Perspectives on Artistic Research and Academia* (Amsterdam: Leiden University Press).

Brater, Enoch (1987), *Beyond Minimalism: Beckett's Late Style in the Theatre* (Oxford: Oxford University Press).

(1994), *The Drama in the Text: Beckett's Late Fiction* (New York: Oxford University Press).

(2008), 'From Dada to Didi: Beckett and the Art of His Century', in: *Samuel Beckett Today/Aujourd'hui*, 19.1: 173–86.

Braun, Edward (1998), *Meyerhold: A Revolution in Theatre*, 2nd ed. (London: Methuen Drama).

Brook, Peter [1968] (1996), *The Empty Space* (New York: Simon & Schuster).

(2018), *The Shifting Point: Forty Years of Theatrical Exploration, 1946–87* (London: Bloomsbury).

Brown, Ethan (2007), 'The lower ninth ward meets Samuel Beckett', *The Guardian*, 12 November. URL: www.theguardian.com/world/2007/nov/12/usa.media

Bryden, Mary, ed. (1998), *Samuel Beckett and Music* (Oxford: Clarendon Press).

Cadena, Richard (2013), *Automated Lighting: The Art and Science of Moving Light in Theatre, Live Performance, and Entertainment*, 2nd ed. (London: Taylor & Francis).

Cage, John (1973), *Silence* (Hanover, NH: Wesleyan University Press).

Causey, Matthew (2006), *Theatre and Performance in Digital Culture: From Simulation to Embeddedness* (Oxon: Routledge).

Causey, Matthew and Fintan Walsh, eds. (2013), *Performance, Identity, and the Neo-Political Subject* (New York and Oxon: Routledge).

Chaikin, Joseph (1972), *The Presence of the Actor* (New York: Atheneum).

Channel 4 (2017), 'Samuel Beckett's *Not I* performed by an actor with Tourette's syndrome', 5 August. URL: www.channel4.com/news/samuel-becketts-not-i-performed-by-an-actor-with-tourettes-syndrome.

Coetzee, J. M. (1973), 'Samuel Beckett's Lessness: An Exercise in Decomposition', in: *Computers and the Humanities*, 7.4: 195–8. DOI:10.100 7/BF02403929

Cohn, Ruby (1980), *Just Play: Beckett's Theatre* (Princeton: Princeton University Press).

Connor, Steven (2006), *Samuel Beckett: Repetition, Theory and Text*, revised ed. (Aurora, CO: Davies Group).

    (2014), *Beckett, Modernism, and the Material Imagination* (Cambridge: Cambridge University Press).

Consultancy.UK (2018), 'Virtual and Augmented Reality Market to Boom to $170 Billion by 2022', 12 July. URL: www.consultancy.uk/news/17876/virtual-and-augmented-reality-market-to-boom-to-170-billion-by-2022

Crawley, Peter (2016), 'Pan Pan Co-founder Aedín Cosgrove Gets into the Mind of Samuel Beckett', *Irish Times*, 21 April. URL: www.irishtimes.com/culture/stage/pan-pan-co-founder-aed%C3%ADn-cosgrove-gets-into-the-mind-of -samuel-beckett-1.2619535

Crease, Robert (1993), *The Play of Nature: Experimentation as Performance* (Bloomington: Indiana University Press).

Crisafulli, Fabrizio (2013), *Active Light: Issues of Light in Contemporary Theatre* (Dublin: Artdigiland).

Daly, John (2017), 'Palace of Theatrical Delights – The Everyman Celebrates 120 Years', *Irish Examiner*, 31 March. URL: www.irishexaminer.com/life

style/artsfilmtv/palace-of-theatrical-delights–the-everyman-celebrates
-120-years-446540.html

Dickson, Andrew (2008), '"Fragments" Review', *The Guardian*, 29 August.
URL: www.theguardian.com/stage/2008/aug/29/theatre.beckett.fragments

Dinçel, Burç İdem (2013), 'The Voyage of *The Trojan Women*: From Euripides
to Sartre and from Sartre to Theatre Research Laboratory', in: *Tiyatro
Araştırmaları Dergisi*, 36.2: 21–59.

(2019), 'Translating the Tragic: Mimetic Transformation of Attic Tragedies
on the Contemporary Stage', PhD dissertation, Trinity College Dublin.

Drew, Elizabeth and Mads Haahr (2002), '*Lessness*: Randomness, Consciousness
and Meaning', Conference paper. URL: www.random.org/lessness/paper/

Feldman, Matthew (2010), 'Beckett, Sartre and Phenomenology,' *Limit(e) Beckett*
0, 1–26. URL: www.limitebeckett.paris-sorbonne.fr/zero/feldman.html

(2015), *Falsifying Beckett* (Stuttgart: Ibidem).

Fifield, Peter (2015), 'Samuel Beckett with, in, and around Philosophy', in: Van
Hulle (2015), 145–57.

Firestein, Stuart (2015), *Failure: Why Science Is so Successful* (Oxford: Oxford
University Press).

Fischer-Lichte, Erika (2009), 'Interweaving Cultures in Performance: Different
States of Being In-Between', in: *New Theatre Quarterly*, 25.4: 391–401.

Fitzgerald, Des and Felicity Callard (2015), 'Social Science and Neuroscience
Beyond Interdisciplinarity: Experimental Entanglements, *Theory, Culture
& Society*, 32.1: 3–32. DOI:10.1177/0263276414537319

Fowler, Benjamin, ed. (2018), *4 x 45 / The Theatre of Katie Mitchell* (New York
and Oxon: Routledge).

Freeman, John (2010), *Blood, Sweat and Theory: Research Through Practice in
Performance* (Faringdon: Libri).

Freire, Paulo [1968] (1971), *Pedagogy of the Oppressed*, trans. by Myra
Bergman Ramos (New York: Herder and Herder).

Frodeman, Robert, ed. (2010), *The Oxford Handbook of Interdisciplinarity*
(Oxford: Oxford University Press).

Frost, Everett (2009), 'Preface', in Beckett (2009a), vii–xxiii.

Garner, Stanton B. (1994), *Bodied Spaces: Phenomenology and Performance in
Contemporary Drama* (Ithaca: Cornell University Press).

Gendron, Sarah (2008), *Repetition, Difference, and Knowledge in the Work of
Samuel Beckett, Jacques Derrida, and Gilles Deleuze* (Bern: Peter Lang).

Goodlander, Jennifer (2008), 'Review of *Beckett Shorts* dir. JoAnne Akalaitis',
in: *Theatre Journal*, 60.3: 463–65. URL: www.jstor.org/stable/40211075

Gontarski, S. E. (1985), *The Intent of Undoing in Samuel Beckett's Dramatic
Texts* (Bloomington: Indiana University Press).

Gontarski, S. E., ed. (2010), *A Companion to Samuel Beckett* (Chichester: Wiley-Blackwell).

Government of Canada (2015), *RIC-22: General Radiotelephone Operating Procedures*. URL: www.ic.gc.ca/eic/site/smt-gst.nsf/eng/sf00033.html

Graham, Katherine (2016), 'Active roles of light in performance design', in: *Theatre and Performance Design*, 2.1–2:73–81. DOI:10.1080/23322551.2016.1178006

    (2018a), 'Scenographic Light: Towards an Understanding of Expressive Light in Performance', PhD dissertation, University of Leeds.

    (2018b), 'In the Shadow of a Dancer: Light as Dramaturgy in Contemporary Performance', in: *Contemporary Theatre Review* 28.2: 196–209. DOI:10.1080/10486801.2017.1412953

Hadley, Bree (2014), *Disability, Public Space Performance and Spectatorship* (London: Palgrave McMillan).

Hadley, Bree and Donna McDonald, eds. (2018), *The Routledge Handbook of Disability Arts, Culture, and Media* (London: Routledge).

Halberstam, Judith (2011), *The Queer Art of Failure* (Durham, NC: Duke University Press).

Hall, Peter (2000), *Peter Hall's Diaries: The Story of a Dramatic Battle* (London: Oberon).

Hann, Rachel (2018), *Beyond Scenography* (London: Routledge).

Harding, James (2013), *The Ghosts of the Avant-Garde: Exorcising Experimental Theatre and Performance* (Ann Arbor: University of Michigan Press).

Harmon, Maurice, ed. (1998), *No Author Better Served: The Correspondence of Samuel Beckett and Alan Schneider* (Cambridge MA: Harvard University Press).

Harvie, Jen (2009), *Theatre and the City* (Houndmills: Palgrave Macmillan).

Haughton, Miriam (2014), 'From Laundries to Labour Camps: Staging Ireland's "Rule of Silence" in Anu Productions' *Laundry*', in: *Modern Drama* 57.1: 65–93. DOI:10.3138/md.0595R

Hegarty-Lovett, Judy (2018), 'Gare St. Lazare Ireland', Transdisciplinary Beckett, Mexico City, 9 November. URL: www.youtube.com/watch?v=nft5Q6MMWfA

Heron, Jonathan (2018), 'End/Lessness', in: *Contemporary Theatre Review*, 'Interventions', 28.1. URL: www.contemporarytheatrereview.org/2018/end-lessness

Heron, Jonathan and Nicholas Johnson (2017), 'Critical Pedagogies and the Theatre Laboratory', in: *Research in Drama Education*, 22.2: 282–87. DOI:10.1080/13569783.2017.1293513

Heron, Jonathan and Nicholas Johnson, with Burç Idem Dinçel, Gavin Quinn, Sarah Jane Scaife, and Áine Josephine Tyrrell (2014), 'The Samuel Beckett Laboratory 2013', in: *Journal of Beckett Studies* 23.1: 73–94. DOI:10.3366/jobs.2014.0087.

Heron, Jonathan and Baz Kershaw (2018), 'On PAR: A Dialogue about Performance-as-Research' in: *Performance as Research: Knowledge, Methods, Impact* ed. by Annette Arlander, Bruce Barton, Melanie Dreyer-Lude, and Ben Spatz (London: Routledge), 20–31.

Herren, Graley (2007), *Samuel Beckett's Plays on Film and Television* (New York: Palgrave Macmillan). DOI:10.1007/978-1-137-10908-8

Higgins, Charlotte (2016), 'Katie Mitchell, British Theatre's Queen in Exile', *The Guardian*, 14 January.

Houston Jones, David (2016), *Installation Art and the Practices of Archivalism* (New York and Oxon: Routledge).

Ingold, Tim (2000), *The Perception of the Environment: Essays on Livelihood, Dwelling and Skill* (London and New York: Routledge).

Jakobson, Roman (1987), *Language in Literature*, ed. by Krystyna Pomorska and Stephen Rudy (Cambridge, MA: Harvard University Press).

Jaleshgari, Ramin P. (1996), 'Simultaneously and Continuously, Beckett Joins 21st Century', *New York Times*, 25 February.

Johnson, Nicholas (2013), 'Performative Criticism: Beckett and Duthuit', in: *Journal of Art Historiography*, 9: 1–10.

(2016), '"The Neatness of Identifications": Transgressing Beckett's Genres in Ireland and Northern Ireland, 2000–2015', in: McTighe and Tucker, 185–202.

(2018), '"Void cannot go": Trauma and Actor Process in the Theatre of Samuel Beckett', in: *Beckett and Trauma*, ed. by M. Tanaka, Y. Tajiri, and M. Tsushima, (Manchester: Manchester University Press), 46–68. DOI:10.7765/9781526121356.00008

Johnson, Nicholas and Brenda O'Connell (2014), 'Three Dialogues on Enniskillen', in: *The Beckett Circle*, Spring.

Johnson, Nicholas and Néill O'Dwyer (2018), 'Virtual Play: Beckettian Experiments in Virtual Reality,' in: *Contemporary Theatre Review*, 'Interventions', 28.1. URL: www.contemporarytheatrereview.org/2018/beckettian-experiments-in-virtual-reality/

Jones, Jonathan (2002), 'Steenbeckett', *The Guardian*, 16 February.

Kalb, Jonathan (1989), *Beckett in Performance* (Cambridge: Cambridge University Press).

Kaye, Nick (2000), *Site-Specific Art: Performance, Place, and Documentation* (London and New York: Routledge).

(2009), 'Disjunction: Performing Media Space', in: Riley and Hunter, 128–30.

Kennedy, Dennis (1993), *Foreign Shakespeare: Contemporary Performance* (Cambridge: Cambridge University Press).

Kirby, Michael (1965), 'The New Theatre', in: *Tulane Drama Review*, 10.2: 23–43.

(1972), 'On Acting and Not-Acting', in: *The Drama Review*, 16.1: 3–15. DOI:10.2307/1144724.

Knorr-Cetina, Karin (1999), *Epistemic Cultures: How the Sciences Make Knowledge* (Cambridge, MA: Harvard University Press).

Knowles, Ric (2017), *Performing the Intercultural City* (Ann Arbor: University of Michigan Press).

Knowlson, James (1987), 'Beckett as Director: The Manuscript Production Notebooks and Critical Interpretation', in: *Modern Drama*, 30.4: 451–65. DOI:10.1353/mdr.1987.0057

(1996), *Damned to Fame: The Life of Samuel Beckett* (New York: Simon & Schuster).

Knowlson, James and Elizabeth Knowlson (2006), *Beckett Remembering / Remembering Beckett* (London: Bloomsbury).

Kuppers, Petra [2004] (2013), *Disability and Contemporary Performance: Bodies on the Edge* (London and New York: Routledge).

(2014), *Studying Disability Arts and Culture: An Introduction* (Houndmills: Palgrave Macmillan).

Latour, Bruno and Steve Woolgar (1979), *Laboratory Life: The Construction of Scientific Facts* (Beverly Hills, CA: Sage)

Laws, Catherine (2005), 'Beckett and Kurtág', in: *Samuel Beckett Today / Aujourd'hui*, 15, 241–56.

(2007), Special Issue: 'On Beckett', *Performance Research*, 12.1.

(2014), 'Beckett in New Musical Composition', in: *Journal of Beckett Studies* 23.1, 54–72. DOI:10.3366.jobs.2014.0086.

Le Feuvre, Lisa, ed. (2010), *Failure* (Cambridge, MA: MIT Press).

Lehmann, Hans-Thies (2005), *Posdramatisches Theater* (Frankfurt am Main: Verlag der Autoren).

Leroi-Gourhan, André (1993), *Gesture and Speech*, trans. by Anna Bostock Berger (Cambridge, MA: MIT Press).

Machon, Josephine (2013), *Immersive Theatres: Intimacy and Immediacy in Contemporary Performance* (Houndmills: Palgrave Macmillan).

Mackrell, Judith (2015), 'Maguy Marin's May B Review – Beckett's Derelicts Go Searching for Cakes and Sex', *The Guardian*, 28 July. URL: www.theguardian.com/stage/2015/jul/28/maguy-marin-may-b-review-beckett

Marranca, Bonnie (1977), *The Theatre of Images* (New York: PAJ Publications).

Maude, Ulrika (2009), *Beckett, Technology and the Body* (Cambridge: Cambridge University Press).

(2015), 'Beckett, Body and Mind', in: Van Hulle (2015), 170–84.

McCarthy, Sean (2009), 'Giving Sam a Second Life: Beckett's Plays in the Age of Convergent Media,' in: *Texas Studies in Literature and Language*, 51.1: 102–17.

McKinney, Joslin and Scott Palmer, eds. (2017), *Scenography Expanded: An Introduction to Contemporary Performance Design* (London and New York: Bloomsbury Methuen).

McMillan, Dougald and Martha Fehsenfeld (1988), *Beckett in the Theatre* (London and New York: Calder and Riverrun).

McMullan, Anna (1993), *Theatre on Trial: Samuel Beckett's Later Drama* (London: Routledge).

(1994), 'Beckett as Director', in: *Cambridge Companion to Samuel Beckett*, ed. by John Pilling (Cambridge: Cambridge University Press), 196–208.

(2010), *Performing Embodiment in Samuel Beckett's Drama* (New York and Oxon: Routledge).

(2016), 'Staging Beckett in Ireland: Scenographic Remains', in: McTighe and Tucker, 103–19.

McMullan, Anna and Graham Saunders (2018), 'Staging Beckett and Contemporary Theatre and Performance Cultures', in: *Contemporary Theatre Review* 28.1: 3–9. DOI:10.1080/10486801.2017.1405393

McTighe, Trish (2018), 'In Caves, in Ruins: Place as Archive at the Happy Days International Beckett Festival', in: *Contemporary Theatre Review* 28.1: 27–38. DOI:10.1080/10486801.2017.1405391

McTighe, Trish and David Tucker, eds. (2016), *Staging Beckett in Ireland and Northern Ireland* (London and New York: Bloomsbury).

McTighe, Trish and Kathryn White (2018), 'Beckett, Ireland and the Biographical Festival: A Symposium', in: *Contemporary Theatre Review*, 'Interventions', 28.1. URL: www.contemporarytheatrereview.org/2018/beckett-and-the-biographical-festival/

Mitchell, Katie and Anna McMullan (2018), 'Katie Mitchell on Staging Beckett', in: *Contemporary Theatre Review* 28.1: 127–132. DOI:10.1080/10486801.2018.1426822

Nora, Pierre (1989), 'Between Memory and History: Les Lieux de Mémoire', *Representations*, No. 26 (Spring), pp. 7–24.

Oppenheim, Lois (1997), *Directing Beckett* (Ann Arbor: University of Michigan Press).

O'Toole, Fintan (2013), 'Culture Shock: Two Samuel Beckett Plays in a Car Park? Unmissable', *Irish Times*, 21 September.

Palmer, Scott (2013), *Light: Readings in Theatre Practice* (Houndmills: Palgrave Macmillan).

Paraskeva, Anthony (2017), *Samuel Beckett and Cinema* (London and New York: Bloomsbury).

Pavis, Patrice (2010), 'Intercultural Theatre Today', in: *Forum Modernes Theater*, 25.1: 5–15.

Pearson, Mike (2010), *Site-Specific Performance* (Basingstoke: Palgrave Macmillan).

Pountney, Rosemary (1988), *Theatre of Shadows: Samuel Beckett's Drama 1956–76* (Buckinghamshire: Colin Smythe).

Quinn, Gavin (2011), 'Pan Pan: A Theatre of Ideas', *Irish Theatre Magazine*. URL: http://itmarchive.ie/web/Features/Current/Pan-Pan–A-theatre-of-ideas.aspx.html

Rabaté, Jean-Michel (2010), 'Philosophizing with Beckett: Adorno and Badiou', in: Gontarski (2010), 97–117.

Reginio, Robert, David Houston Jones, and Katherine Weiss, eds. (2017), *Samuel Beckett and Contemporary Art* (Stuttgart: Ibidem).

Rickson, Ian (2014), 'The Feeling in the Play: An Interview with Ian Rickson', with Jonathan Heron, in: *Journal of Beckett Studies*, 23.1: 95–101. DOI:10.3366/jobs.2014.0088

Ridout, Nicholas (2006), *Stage Fright, Animals, and Other Theatrical Problems* (Cambridge: Cambridge University Press).

Riley, Shannon Rose and Lynette Hunter, eds. (2009), *Mapping Landscapes for Performance as Research: Scholarly Acts and Creative Cartographies* (Houndmills: Palgrave Macmillan).

Roach, Joseph (1985), *The Player's Passion: Studies in the Science of Acting* (Newark: University of Delaware Press).

(1996), *Cities of the Dead: Circum-Atlantic Performance* (New York: Columbia University Press).

Robbins Dudeck, Theresa (2013), *Keith Johnstone: A Critical Biography* (London and New York: Bloomsbury).

Rottenberg, Anda (2017), 'Pursuing Meaning, Fleeing Meaning', Pirelli Hangar Bicocca, Milan. URL: https://nordenhake.com/artists/miroslaw-balka

Scaife, Sarah Jane (2013), 'The Culturally Inscribed Body and Spaces of Performance in Samuel Beckett's Theatre', PhD Dissertation, University of Reading.

(2016), 'Practice in Focus: Beckett in the City', in: McTighe and Tucker, 153–67.

(2018), 'Situating the Audience – Performance Encounter *Beckett in the City: The Women Speak*,' in: *Contemporary Theatre Review*, 28.1: 114–26. DOI:10.1080/10486801.2017.1405392

Schechner, Richard (2013), *Performance Studies: An Introduction*, 3rd ed. (New York and Oxon: Routledge).

Schneider, Alan and Richard Schechner (1965), 'Reality Is Not Enough', in: *Tulane Drama Review*, 9.3: 118–52. URL: www.jstor.org/stable/1125051

Shaw, Fiona (2007a), 'Buried in Beckett', *The Guardian*, 23 January. URL: www.theguardian.com/theguardian/2007/jan/23/features11.g21

(2007b), 'Breaking the Silence', *The Guardian*, 25 August. URL: www.theguardian.com/books/2007/aug/25/theatre.samuelbeckett

Shepherd, Simon and Mick Wallis (2004), *Drama/Theatre/Performance* (London: Routledge).

Simondon, Gilbert (1958), *Du mode de l'existence des objets techniques* (Paris: Aubier).

Singleton, Brian (2013), 'ANU Productions and Site-Specific Performance: The Politics of Space and Place', in: *That Was Us: Contemporary Irish Theatre and Performance*, ed. by Fintan Walsh (London: Oberon), 21–36.

(2016a), 'Beckett and the Non-Place in Irish Performance', in: McTighe and Tucker, 169–84.

(2016b), *ANU Productions: The Monto Cycle* (London: Palgrave Macmillan). DOI:10.1057/978-1-349-95133-8

Stanislavski, Konstantin (2008), *An Actor's Work*, trans. by Jean Benedetti (London and New York: Routledge).

Stiegler, Bernard (1998), *Technics and Time, 1: The Fault of Epimetheus*, trans. by Richard Beardsworth and George Collins (Stanford: Stanford University Press).

(2014). *Symbolic Misery, Volume 1: The Hyperindustrial Epoch* (Oxford: Polity).

Tate Modern (2009), 'The Unilever Series: Miroslaw Balka: How It Is', URL: www.tate.org.uk/whats-on/tate-modern/exhibition/unilever-series/unilever-series-miroslaw-balka-how-it

Taylor, Diana (2003), *The Archive and the Repertoire: Performing Cultural Memory in the Americas* (Durham, NC: Duke University Press).

Thom, Jessica (2012), *Welcome to Biscuit Land: A Year in the Life of Touretteshero* (London: Souvenir Press).

Tubridy, Derval (2014), 'Samuel Beckett and Performance Art', in: *Journal of Beckett Studies* 23.1: 34–53. DOI:10.3366/jobs.2014.0085

(2018), 'Theatre and Installation: Perspectives on Beckett', in: *Contemporary Theatre Review* 28.1: 68–81. DOI:10.1080/10486801.2017.1405394

Uhlmann, Anthony (2010), 'Beckett and Philosophy', in: Gontarski (2010), 84–96.

Van Hulle, Dirk, ed. (2013), *Modern Manuscripts: The Extended Mind and Creative Undoing from Darwin to Beckett and Beyond* (London: Bloomsbury).

(2015), *The New Cambridge Companion to Samuel Beckett* (Cambridge: Cambridge University Press).

Varela, Francisco, Evan Thompson, and Eleanor Rosch (1991), *The Embodied Mind: Cognitive Science and Human Experience* (Cambridge, MA: MIT Press).

Verhulst, Pim (2015), '"There are differences": Variants and Errors in the Texts of Beckett's Radio Plays', in: *Journal of Beckett Studies*, 24.1: 57–74. DOI:10.3366/jobs.2015.0120

Weller, Shane (2010), 'Beckett and Ethics', in: Gontarski (2010), 118–29.

White, Gareth (2012), 'On Immersive Theatre', in: *Theatre Research International* 37.3: 221–35. DOI:10.1017/S0307883312000880

Wilkie, Fiona (2002), 'Mapping the Terrain: A Survey of Site-Specific Performance in Britain', in: *New Theatre Quarterly* 18.2: 140–60. DOI:10.1017/S0266464X02000234

Williams, David and Lorna Marshall (2000), 'Peter Brook: Transparency and the Invisible Network,' in: *Twentieth Century Actor Training*, ed. by Alison Hodge (London and New York: Routledge), 174–90.

Wilson, Robert (2014), 'Automatic in the Muscle: An Interview with Robert Wilson', with Nicholas Johnson, in: *Journal of Beckett Studies*, 23.1: 101–6. DOI:10.3366/jobs.2014.0089

Worth, Katharine (1999), *Samuel Beckett's Theatre: Life Journeys* (Oxford: Oxford University Press).

Zarrilli, Phillip (2001), 'Negotiating Performance Epistemologies: Knowledges "About", "In" and "For"', in: *Studies in Theatre and Performance*, 21.1: 31–46. DOI:10.1386/stap.21.1.31

(2002), 'The Metaphysical Studio', in: *TDR*, 46.2: 157–70.

(2018), '"Meditations" on Loss: Beyond Discourses of Pain and Torture in the Work of the Beckett Actor,' in: *Contemporary Theatre Review*, 28.1: 95–113. DOI:10.1080/10486801.2017.1405949.

Acknowledgements

First, we wish to thank the general series editors, as well as the entire team at Cambridge University Press, for the opportunity to explore these questions in print and for their ongoing support of our work.

The roots of this volume are deeply embedded in the collaboration that led to the foundation of the Samuel Beckett Laboratory in 2013, and there are untraceable insights within our writing here that are the product of collective investigations in that space. Thus, we thank all participants, guest artists, designers, technicians, and academics who have contributed to the Lab events over the past six years.

We are grateful to our institutions, Trinity College Dublin and the University of Warwick, which have also supported our efforts in countless ways – travel funding, project funding, and research leave uppermost – without which we would not have been able to complete this task. In particular, we recognise the supportive insights of our academic colleagues and our students. The staff of the Institute for Advanced Teaching and Learning (IATL) at the University of Warwick and the Trinity Long Room Hub, which hosts and supports the Trinity Centre for Beckett Studies at Trinity College Dublin, have been helpful and understanding throughout the project's development.

We thank our mentors and teachers, especially remembering those who are no longer with us. We thank our fellow travellers, co-authors, and collaborators in the wider Beckett and theatre studies communities, who challenge and sharpen our ideas in the most generous and productive ways. We thank our partners, families, and friends, who give us immeasurable support in maintaining, in the midst of work, a life worthy of the name.

Many of the artists discussed in this volume gave freely of their time to speak about their work, opened their rehearsal rooms to us, and made available archival copies of their projects, their writing, or their notes. The artists who continue to create Beckett's living legacy are braving a difficult and important path, and we owe them a great debt not only as scholars or artists, but also as members of their audience. We thank them collectively here, and we dedicate this work to them.

Cambridge Elements ≡

Beckett Studies

Dirk Van Hulle
University of Oxford
Dirk Van Hulle is Professor of Bibliography and Modern Book History at the University of Oxford and director of the Centre for Manuscript Genetics at the University of Antwerp.

Mark Nixon
University of Reading
Mark Nixon is Associate Professor in Modern Literature at the University of Reading and the Co-Director of the Beckett International Foundation.

About the Series
This series presents cutting-edge research by distinguished and emerging scholars, providing space for the most relevant debates informing Beckett studies as well as neglected aspects of his work. In times of technological development, religious radicalism, unprecedented migration, gender fluidity, environmental and social crisis, Beckett's works find increased resonance. Elements in Beckett Studies is a key resource for readers interested in the current state of the field.

Cambridge Elements $\equiv$

Beckett Studies

Elements in the Series

Experimental Beckett: Contemporary Performance Practices
Nicholas E. Johnson and Jonathan Heron

Postcognitivist Beckett
Olga Beloborodova

A full series listing is available at: www.cambridge.org/eibs

www.ingramcontent.com/pod-product-compliance
Ingram Content Group UK Ltd.
Pitfield, Milton Keynes, MK11 3LW, UK
UKHW020454010325
455719UK00016B/588